EMERGENCY EXIT

WORLD PERSPECTIVES

Volumes already published

WORLD PERSPECTIVES · *Volume Thirty-nine*

Planned and Edited by RUTH NANDA ANSHEN

EMERGENCY EXIT

IGNAZIO SILONE

1817

HARPER & ROW, PUBLISHERS
NEW YORK, EVANSTON, AND LONDON

"Visit to a Prisoner," "Judith's Tresses," "Encounter with a Strange Priest," "Polikushka," "Emergency Exit," "The Situation of the 'Ex,'" "The Choice of Companions," "The Lesson of Budapest," and "The Painful Return" were translated from the Italian by Harvey Fergusson II.

This book was first published in Italy under the title *Uscita Di Sicurezza.* Copyright © 1965 by Vallecchi Editore Firenze.

FIRST EDITION

LIBRARY OF CONGRESS CATALOG CARD NUMBER: 65-14658

I-S

Contents

Contents

World Perspectives
What This Series Means

It is the thesis of *World Perspectives* that man is in the process of developing a new consciousness which, in spite of his apparent spiritual and moral captivity, can eventually lift the human race above and beyond the fear, ignorance, and isolation which beset it today. It is to this nascent consciousness, to this concept of man born out of a universe perceived through a fresh vision of reality, that *World Perspectives* is dedicated.

Man has entered a new era of evolutionary history, one in which rapid change is a dominant consequence. He is contending with a fundamental change, since he has intervened in the evolutionary process. He must now better appreciate this fact and then develop the wisdom to direct the process toward his fulfillment rather than toward his destruction. As he learns to apply his understanding of the physical world for practical purposes, he is, in reality, extending his innate capacity and augmenting his ability and his need to communicate as well as his ability to think and to create. And as a result, he is substituting a goal-directed evolutionary process in his struggle against environmental hardship for the slow, but effective, biological evolution which produced modern man through mutation and natural selection. By intelligent intervention in the evolutionary process man has greatly accelerated and greatly expanded the range of his possibilities. But he has not changed the basic fact that it remains a trial and error process, with the danger of taking paths that lead to sterility of mind and heart, moral apathy and intellectual inertia; and even producing social dinosaurs unfit to live in an evolving world.

Only those spiritual and intellectual leaders of our epoch who have a paternity in this extension of man's horizons are invited to participate in this Series: those who are aware of the truth that beyond the divisiveness among men there exists a primordial unitive power since we are all bound together by a common humanity more fundamental than any unity of dogma; those who recognize that the centrifugal force which has scattered and atomized mankind must be replaced by an integrating structure and process capable of bestowing meaning and purpose on existence; those who realize that science itself, when not inhibited by the limitations of its own methodology, when chastened and humbled, commits man to an indeterminate range of yet undreamed consequences that may flow from it.

This Series endeavors to point to a reality of which scientific theory has revealed only one aspect. It is the commitment to this reality that lends universal intent to a scientist's most original and solitary thought. By acknowledging this frankly we shall restore science to the great family of human aspirations by which men hope to fulfill themselves in the world community as thinking and sentient beings. For our problem is to discover a principle of differentiation and yet relationship lucid enough to justify and to purify scientific, philosophic and all other knowledge, both discursive and intuitive, by accepting their interdependence. This is the crisis in consciousness made articulate through the crisis in science. This is the new awakening.

Each volume presents the thought and belief of its author and points to the way in which religion, philosophy, art, science, economics, politics and history may constitute that form of human activity which takes the fullest and most precise account of variousness, possibility, complexity and difficulty. Thus *World Perspectives* endeavors to define that ecumenical power of the mind and heart which enables man through his mysterious greatness to re-create his life.

This Series is committed to a re-examination of all those sides of human endeavor which the specialist was taught to believe he could safely leave aside. It attempts to show the structural kinship between subject and object; the indwelling of the one in the other. It interprets present and past events impinging on human life in our growing World Age and envisages what man may yet attain when summoned by an unbending inner necessity to the quest of what is most exalted in him. Its purpose is to offer new vistas in terms of world and human development while refusing to betray the intimate correlation between universality and individuality, dynamics and form, freedom and destiny. Each author deals with the increasing realization that spirit and nature are not separate and apart; that intuition and reason must regain their importance as the means of perceiving and fusing inner being with outer reality.

World Perspectives endeavors to show that the conception of wholeness, unity, organism is a higher and more concrete conception than that of matter and energy. Thus an enlarged meaning of life, of biology, not as it is revealed in the test tube of the laboratory but as it is experienced within the organism of life itself, is attempted in this Series. For the principle of life consists in the tension which connects spirit with the realm of matter, symbiotically joined. The element of life is dominant in the very texture of nature, thus rendering life, biology, a transempirical science. The laws of life have their origin beyond their mere physical manifestations and compel us to consider their spiritual source. In fact, the widening of the conceptual framework has not only served to restore order within the respective branches of knowledge, but has also disclosed analogies in man's position regarding the analysis and synthesis of experience in apparently separated domains of knowledge, suggesting the possibility of an ever more embracing objective description of the meaning of life.

Knowledge, it is shown in these books, no longer consists in a manipulation of man and nature as opposite forces, nor in the reduction of data to mere statistical order, but is a means of liberating mankind from the destructive power of fear, pointing the way toward the goal of the rehabilitation of the human will and the rebirth of faith and confidence in the human person.

The works published also endeavor to reveal that the cry for patterns, systems and authorities is growing less insistent as the desire grows stronger in both East and West for the recovery of a dignity, integrity and self-realization which are the inalienable rights of man, who may now guide change by means of conscious purpose in the light of rational experience.

The volumes in this Series endeavor to demonstrate that only in a society in which awareness of the problems of science exists, can its discoveries start great waves of change in human culture, and in such a manner that these discoveries may deepen and not erode the sense of universal human community. The differences in the disciplines, their epistemological exclusiveness, the variety of historical experiences, the differences of traditions, of cultures, of languages, of the arts, should be protected and preserved. But the interrelationship and unity of the whole should at the same time be accepted.

The authors of *World Perspectives* are of course aware that the ultimate answers to the hopes and fears which pervade modern society rest on the moral fiber of man, and on the wisdom and responsibility of those who promote the course of its development. But moral decisions cannot dispense with an insight into the interplay of the objective elements which offer and limit the choices made. Therefore an understanding of what the issues are, though not a sufficient condition, is a necessary prerequisite for directing action toward constructive solutions.

Other vital questions explored relate to problems of international understanding as well as to problems dealing with prejudice and the resultant tensions and antagonisms. The growing perception and responsibility of our World Age point to the new reality that the individual person and the collective person supplement and integrate each other; that the thrall of totalitarianism of both left and right has been shaken in the universal desire to recapture the authority of truth and human totality. Mankind can finally place its trust not in a proletarian authoritarianism, not in a secularized humanism, both of which have

betrayed the spiritual property right of history, but in a sacra-
mental brotherhood and in the unity of knowledge. This new
consciousness has created a widening of human horizons beyond
every parochialism, and a revolution in human thought comparable to the basic assumption, among the ancient Greeks, of
the sovereignty of reason; corresponding to the great effulgence
of the moral conscience articulated by the Hebrew prophets;
analogous to the fundamental assertions of Christianity; or to
the beginning of the new scientific era, the era of the science of
dynamics, the experimental foundations of which were laid by
Galileo in the Renaissance.

An important effort of this Series is to re-examine the contradictory meanings and applications which are given today to
such terms as democracy, freedom, justice, love, peace, brotherhood and God. The purpose of such inquiries is to clear the way
for the foundation of a genuine *world* history not in terms of
nation or race or culture but in terms of man in relation to
God, to himself, his fellow man and the universe, that reach
beyond immediate self-interest. For the meaning of the World
Age consists in respecting man's hopes and dreams which lead to
a deeper understanding of the basic values of all peoples.

World Perspectives is planned to gain insight into the meaning of man, who not only is determined by history but who also
determines history. History is to be understood as concerned
not only with the life of man on this planet but as including
also such cosmic influences as interpenetrate our human world.
This generation is discovering that history does not conform to
the social optimism of modern civilization and that the organization of human communities and the establishment of freedom and peace are not only intellectual achievements but
spiritual and moral achievements as well, demanding a cherish-
ing of the wholeness of human personality, the "unmediated
wholeness of feeling and thought," and constituting a never-
ending challenge to man, emerging from the abyss of meaning-
lessness and suffering, to be renewed and replenished in the
totality of his life.

Justice itself, which has been "in a state of pilgrimage and crucifixion" and now is being slowly liberated from the grip of social and political demonologies in the East as well as in the West, begins to question its own premises. The modern revolutionary movements which have challenged the sacred institutions of society by protecting social injustice in the name of social justice are here examined and re-evaluated.

In the light of this, we have no choice but to admit that the un-freedom against which freedom is measured must be retained with it, namely, that the aspect of truth out of which the night view appears to emerge, the darkness of our time, is as little abandonable as is man's subjective advance. Thus the two sources of man's consciousness are inseparable, not as dead but as living and complementary, an aspect of that "principle of complementarity" through which Niels Bohr has sought to unite the quantum and the wave, both of which constitute the very fabric of life's radiant energy.

There is in mankind today a counterforce to the sterility and danger of a quantitative, anonymous mass culture; a new, if sometimes imperceptible, spiritual sense of convergence toward human and world unity on the basis of the sacredness of each human person and respect for the plurality of cultures. There is a growing awareness that equality may not be evaluated in mere numerical terms but is proportionate and analogical in its reality. For when equality is equated with interchangeability, individuality is negated and the human person extinguished.

We stand at the brink of an age of a world in which human life presses forward to actualize new forms. The false separation of man and nature, of time and space, of freedom and security, is acknowledged, and we are faced with a new vision of man in his organic unity and of history offering a richness and diversity of quality and majesty of scope hitherto unprecedented. In relating the accumulated wisdom of man's spirit to the new reality of the World Age, in articulating its thought and belief, *World Perspectives* seeks to encourage a renaissance of hope in society and of pride in man's decision as to what his destiny will be.

World Perspectives is committed to the recognition that all great changes are preceded by a vigorous intellectual re-evaluation and reorganization. Our authors are aware that the sin of *hubris* may be avoided by showing that the creative process itself is not a free activity if by free we mean arbitrary, or unrelated to cosmic law. For the creative process in the human mind, the developmental process in organic nature and the basic laws of the inorganic realm may be but varied expressions of a universal formative process. Thus *World Perspectives* hopes to show that although the present apocalyptic period is one of exceptional tensions, there is also at work an exceptional movement toward a compensating unity which refuses to violate the ultimate moral power at work in the universe, that very power upon which all human effort must at last depend. In this way we may come to understand that there exists an inherent independence of spiritual and mental growth which, though conditioned by circumstances, is never determined by circumstances. In this way the great plethora of human knowledge may be correlated with an insight into the nature of human nature by being attuned to the wide and deep range of human thought and human experience.

In spite of the infinite obligation of men and in spite of their finite power, in spite of the intransigence of nationalisms, and in spite of the homelessness of moral passions rendered ineffectual by the scientific outlook, beneath the apparent turmoil and upheaval of the present, and out of the transformations of this dynamic period with the unfolding of a world-consciousness, the purpose of *World Perspectives* is to help quicken the "unshaken heart of well-rounded truth" and interpret the significant elements of the World Age now taking shape out of the core of that undimmed continuity of the creative process which restores man to mankind while deepening and enhancing his communion with the universe.

RUTH NANDA ANSHEN

I

Visit to a Prisoner

A small, barefoot, ragged little man, handcuffed between two policemen, was proceeding by fits and starts along the dusty deserted street, as if to the rhythm of a painful dance, perhaps because he was lame or wounded in the foot. Between the two uniformed figures, whose faces looked like death masks in the harsh summer light, the little man had an air of earthy vitality about him, like an animal who had been captured in some ditch. He had a bundle on his back which made a noise like a cicada every time he moved.

This pitiful, farcical sight approached as I was seated on the front stoop with my spelling book on my knees. I was having my first difficulties with vowels and consonants, and here was an unexpected distraction that made me laugh. I looked around for someone to enjoy it with me, and at that moment, from inside the house, I heard my father's heavy footsteps.

"Look how funny he is!" I said to him with a laugh.

My father looked severely at me, dragged me to my feet by the ear and led me to his room. I had never seen him so angry at me.

"What have I done wrong?" I asked him, rubbing my injured ear.

"Never make fun of a man who's been arrested! Never!"

"Why not?"

"Because he can't defend himself. And because he may be innocent. In any case because he's unhappy."

1

Without saying anything more, he left me alone in the room, the victim of a new kind of torment. Vowels and consonants, with their complicated combinations, no longer interested me.

That evening, instead of sending me to bed at the usual time, my father took me to town with him, something which happened only rarely. And instead of staying with his friends at the Farmers' League as he usually did, he went to sit at a table in front of the "gentlemen's" café, where the town's leading citizens were enjoying the cool breeze after a hot day. At the next table, the judge was talking with the municipal doctor.

"What is that man they arrested today accused of?" my father asked the judge, with whom he was on good terms.

"He stole something," answered the judge.

"Where's the thief from? Is he a vagabond? Is he out of work?" my father asked again.

"He's a laborer at the brick factory, and it seems he stole something from the manager," answered the judge. "Did he steal something from you too?"

"That's strange," said my father. "Barefoot and in rags as he was, he looked more like a victim than a thief."

The sight of poor people handcuffed between policemen was common enough on the street where we lived, because all prisoners arrested in the villages in our country had to pass that way. And they had to walk since there was no other way to transport them.

The old part of our town was backed up against a mountain and was overlooked by the ruins of an ancient castle. It consisted of a great rabbit warren of black peasant huts, stables for the animals carved out of the rock, a couple of churches and some uninhabited mansions. But with the increase in population in the last few years, the town was expanding into the valley on both banks of the river, and our street was the principal road to the plain and the Fucino Valley, where draining of the lake had made available lots of good rich land. It was a street of intense and noisy traffic. Not having a durable road bed, it changed appearance with the seasons. It was as treacherous and irregular as the bed of a torrent, and it looked like a wide country road with its numerous ruts, full of mud or snow in the winter and of blinding dust in the summer. The houses along the street, most of them two-storied, were unable to protect themselves from the dust or the noise. They even added to it since their occupants were mostly craftsmen plying their trades.

At the first light of dawn, there began on our street the daily procession of goats, sheep, donkeys, mules, cows, wagons of every description and use, and peasants, making their way down to the plain for the day's work. And every evening until late the same procession of men and animals passed in the opposite direction, showing clear signs of fatigue. In the intervening hours, the space in front of the houses was occupied by the craftsmen—carpenters, shoemakers, smiths, tinkers, wagoners, coopers, and dyers, with the tools of their trade—while long rows of small carts loaded with "red earth" and pulled by mules passed up the street. The "red earth" was extracted by very primitive means from an exhausted bauxite mine dug out of a nearby mountain, and it was on its way to the railroad. No one in our town knew where it was going. Very often, when the weather was bad, one of those wagons got stuck in a rut hidden by the mud. Then the whole column of "red earth" would halt for hours, among the shouts and curses of the carters.

A few years later my father consented to take me with him to Fucino for the first time. This was an important event for me. I had the sensation, all of a sudden, of having become a man. I woke up in the morning when it was still dark, but he had already prepared the oxen and had the wagon drawn up in front of the door of the house. I was also astonished to hear the sound of the loom in the weaving room. Was my mother at work already? She soon came to keep me company while I had my coffee and milk; and she gave me a bit of advice. I remember that she strongly warned me not to sit in the sun once I got to the Fucino Valley. "A lot of people get sunstroke the first time they go out in the country," she said. Then she went with me to the wagon. Every detail added to my anxiety. In the pallid light of dawn, the large shape of the oxen, the crude simplicity of the things loaded up for the day—the plow, the sack of hay, the flasks of water and wine, and the basket of food—and the customary but unexpected crowing of the rooster appeared to me portents of the seriousness of the life into which I was about to be admitted. We had to leave so early because it was about five miles to the middle of the Fucino Valley, where our farmland was located. It was advisable for both us and the oxen to get there before the sun was too high.

An ox cart, obviously, moves about as fast as a man walks. But that slow pace suited my state of mind: that of a boy admitted for the first time to the life of adults. I was watching the peasants in front and in back of us in the line of wagons and animals, and I was trying to act as they did, hiding my emotion. It struck me that even good friends greeted each other with barely a nod of the head. It was a working day and there was no time to stand on ceremony. Nor was I disturbed that my father, lost in thought, said nothing, showing that as far as he was concerned I was no longer a child. One unexpected discovery for me was the view of our town I had as I turned back from the plain. I had never seen it as a whole before, outside myself, with its own valley. I hardly recognized it: a pile of houses jumbled together in a crack in the barren mountain.

As we slowly came into the plain, the crowd of peasants, wagons, mules and donkeys dispersed to the right and left, until we were almost alone. It was only then that my father realized that he had not brought along any tobacco. From the way he acted, I understood that this must be a very serious oversight. How could he spend the whole day in that hot air without smoking? Not even the poorest peasant could make this sacrifice.

The sun was already high and we were too far into the Fucino Valley to think of turning back. I felt especially mortified that my father kept repeating, "I've never forgotten something like that! Never!" Was it my fault then? I was horrified at the thought. My memorable day had suddenly darkened. When we got to the field, my father loosened the oxen from the cart and hitched them to the plow, without saying a word, without even looking at me. The long, dusty, poplar-lined road was deserted, as were the rectangles of fields near ours. There was no hope of finding a friend who would give up some of his tobacco. My father was starting the oxen off behind the plow when he called me.

"Take this coin," he said, "and offer it to everyone who passes in exchange for a cigar or a pinch of snuff."

The sun was already high, and it was unlikely that anyone was still on the road. My father took off his jacket, lifted the iron goad and urged on the oxen in an angry voice. Depressed, I sat on the grassy bank of the canal which separated the field from the road. I could see my father bent over the plow behind the oxen, fading slowly away, then coming back, then going off again, tracing straight, ashen furrows in the earth blackened by burned stubble. The plowing went on silently and regularly, even though the sun was beginning to burn. Around the edge of the field, the gigantic poplars formed a barrier unmoved by a breath of wind. The waters of the canal were turbid, immobile, stagnant. Although I was seated in the shade, I could hardly breathe. I was seized with a vague sense of nausea and sleepiness. I was thinking it would have been better if I had stayed home. But about noon my father's voice roused me from my stupor. A man riding on a small donkey was coming along the road in our direction. It seemed as if he and his donkey were being carried along by the low dense cloud which raised the invisible feet of the animal from the ground. I ran up to him, showed him the coin and proposed the trade, pointing out my father, who had stopped with the oxen halfway along the furrow. The man was a very poor-looking farmer. He had on a few dirty rags which left some of his body exposed, and he was wearing some broken-down shoes tied with pieces of twine.

"I haven't got a whole cigar," he answered me. "Just about half a one."

"Fine," I said to him, running along beside the donkey, "take this and give me what you have, please."

"And why should I go the whole day without a smoke?" he answered. "Why's your father better than me?"

"My father's no better than you are," I explained. "But something like this can make him go without speaking until tomorrow."

"Too bad for him," the man answered. "Who'll believe it?"

I continued to trot along beside the donkey, but I was beginning to lose hope. How was I going to get that piece of cigar? I looked at the man with pleading eyes, but he was watching me with a sneer—whether of scorn or pity I could not tell. I had never before been that close to so thin and dried-up a man.

"We've got some nice food in our basket," I told him. "If you like, I'll give you my share. And there's some cool wine from our vineyard. Stop a minute, and come see."

The man couldn't be moved. He even seemed to be enjoying himself. It almost made me cry.

"Please," I was repeating to him. "Please."

"Here," he suddenly said, handing me a bit of cigar. "I'll give it to you."

"You won't accept the money? Why?"

"Either you give half a cigar or you don't."

I did not insist because I was in too much of a hurry to make a good impression on my father.

"That's funny," my father said, after I had told him of my good luck with the man. "You should have at least asked his name."

Several years passed. One evening I was sitting on the threshold of the house with the *Fables* of Fedro on my knees, when I saw the very man who had given me the half-cigar passing by, handcuffed between two policemen. I recognized him immediately and my heart almost stopped. I ran to tell my father about it. He was not home yet. I ran to my grandmother. Then I went to the square. No one had seen him. Finally I found my father in the stable, watering the oxen. I must have looked very upset, because as soon as he saw me he asked whether something awful had happened. "Yes," I answered, and I told him whom I had seen.

The next day was a Sunday. After Mass, coming out of the church, I found my father waiting to take me to the judge as we had agreed.

"You tell him about it," said my father. "After all, you're the one who knows the man."

The judge listened with a smile to my short but impassioned account.

"He was arrested because he stole," he explained when I had finished.

I was astonished. To me the stranger looked less like a thief than a violent madman.

"He probably did something the police and the judge think is stealing," my father tried to explain. "But only God knows what he really did."

The judge kindly gave us a card permitting us to visit the man in jail. My name was written on the card too.

"We'll have to take him some little present," my father proposed on the way. "But what?"

"The best thing would be a cigar," I suggested.

"That's an excellent idea," said my father.

I remember every last detail of that visit since it was the first time I had ever been in a place like that. As soon as I set foot inside it, my heart began to beat so fast it hurt. The guard took us to a stinking little room, which was getting a tiny bit of light from a window protected by bars. He showed us an opening in one of the walls at about the height of a man, through which we could talk to the prisoner. I had to stand on tiptoe to see him. How happy I was when he recognized me at first sight.

1965

II

Judith's Tresses

A traveler coming from Fucino would find at the entrance to our village, between the main street and the river, some narrow, filthy alleys, flanked by very poor one-story huts, alternating with straw bins, stables and pigpens. In one of them lived a young woman named Judith, also called the basket maker, who, continuing in her father's trade, made baskets and hampers from the willow twigs growing along the river. It was a trade in which she made barely enough to keep herself alive.

Judith would have been a completely insignificant little woman, a small, robust brunette, large in the chest and hips, like so many others in our part of the world, had not nature given her an extraordinary head of thick, long hair, which from early childhood covered her entire back down to her hips. Nothing like it had ever been seen around there. This formidable mass of hair gathered around her head looked at a distance like a basket and was in curious contrast with her timid little face, which had the color and shape of a wrinkled potato. It was generally agreed among the women that Judith had found a husband solely on account of her unusual head of hair. Once, they said, a young peasant had hidden himself in a thicket along the river bank, and had watched her while she knelt on the opposite shore to wash it, thinking no one could see her.

Some months after her marriage, her husband like so many others had gone to America, taking along as a good-luck piece a bundle of his wife's hair, since at that time it was not considered

8

proper for a young lady to have herself photographed. His hope was to save enough so that on his return he could buy a field and if he was lucky, maybe a garden too, or a bit of a vineyard. His first letters were very faithful, and he soon sent the first few dollars. But thereafter he stopped sending any news of himself. It was a time of tribulation and increasing anxiety for the unhappy Judith. She passed the monotonous days waiting in vain for the postman or in church. Her eyes were always red from weeping. She suffered less from the lack of material help than from the shame of having been so quickly abandoned. One morning, overcome by desolation, she tried to hang herself. The state of depression into which she had fallen was indicated by the fact that before passing the rope around her neck, she had cut off her famous tresses, the one thing she had to be proud of, and thrown them into the fire.

She was saved, in somewhat curious circumstances, by a beggar from no one knew where who had come into the house at that very moment to ask for a piece of bread. The unknown man untied the knot which was pressing against her throat, placed her in a faint on the straw mat and called the neighbor women to help her. No one ever found out who he was, where he came from or how he happened to be begging in a miserable village like ours. In fact, no one paid any attention to him, so he was able to go on about his business unobserved.

As can be imagined, Judith's insane gesture caused a feeling of horror to run through the village. Pity for the poor woman was general, as was contempt for her faithless husband. The misfortune involved everyone to some extent since at that time the greatest resource of the poor families in the region was what emigrants sent from America.

In the large leather sack carried by Nicola the postman, letters with postmarks from Philadelphia or Pittsburgh greatly outnumbered those from Milan or Turin. The most eagerly expected letters naturally were the ones sealed up like the relics of a saint with several wax seals. Many mothers devotedly kissed them and crossed themselves before opening them. They contained money, yes, but they also represented the sacrifices, hard work and faithfulness of the loved ones from whom they came. Because of his job, Nicola the postman had come to play the role, for many families, of Providence's benevolent messenger, which was well suited to his affable, obsequious and pious temperament. He not only brought the letters, but read them to the illiterate recipients, like Judith, and made arrangements with them for answers.

We all knew that Nicola had failed to become a priest only because, from the time he was a boy, he had lacked the money to study theology. But his adherence to the rule of celibacy served to show how seriously he took his vocation. Some reproached him for loving wine a little too much, although he had never been seen in an unruly or vulgar state, even when he was tipsy. My father's opinion, which he never concealed from Nicola, was that there was only one thing to worry about in his character: his preference for drinking alone in his own house. But the postman justified himself on the ground that the status of a "public functionary," of however modest a grade, did not permit him to frequent bars. My father would answer mistrustfully that that was how a priest would argue.

The letters coming from Philadelphia or Pittsburgh did not always bring joy. There was no lack of news about work accidents, which meant ruin for the rest of the victim's life, since there were no workmen's compensation laws then. And there were letters from men who broke off all relations with their families for one reason or another, sometimes because of some malicious gossip they had heard about the conduct of the wives they had left at home. But the behavior of Judith's husband seemed even more strange and unjustified. Not only did the poor woman, who could not have been blamed for a thing, not receive a dollar from him, but she did not receive even two lines of explanation, though it was known, via other emigrants on the same job with him, that he was in good health, earning good money and boasted of sending all his savings home. But to the sorrowful letters of entreaty Judith dictated to the postman, he never deigned to reply.

The mystery was cleared up some weeks after her attempted suicide. (Not, certainly, on her initiative, since from the time she lost her hair she stayed in the house out of shame and lived on the crusts of bread her neighbors brought her.) But a postal inspector—no one knew who called him—discovered with no difficulty that a certain number of insured letters which had regularly arrived at the post office had been pocketed by Nicola the postman. When this news got out, everyone was scandalized. In the circumstances, this was no robbery; it was a sacrilege. Meanwhile, the postman had disappeared without a trace, probably saving himself from a lynching. But the people took a long time to get over their horror. The moral foundation of the community had been brutally outraged. Against his habit, inclined as he was to be an anticonformist, my father shared the general indignation, the more so since the postman's unheard-of disgrace confirmed his well-known mistrust of solitary drinkers.

In the village no one talked of anything else; even the priest spoke of it from the pulpit. Various families took up a collection for the unhappy Judith, while someone undertook the job of writing to her husband. But a new terror now seized Judith's mind, the thought that her man, as soon as he heard what had happened, would come rushing home. What would he think of his wife without her hair? The few women permitted to visit her in her monastic seclusion agreed. They said she was nearly unrecognizable. An old aunt of hers said that she looked more like a monkey than a Christian. But in talking with her they tried, of course, to bring her some comfort. "Your hair will grow back," they would say to her.

"But it'll never be like it was before," Judith would repeat through her sobs. "What good is it for me to keep on living? You should have let me die!"

Meanwhile, there was no trace of the fugitive postman.

"By now he's far away," they said, "and with the money he stole from Judith, he'll get along fine for a long time."

Around that time, some friends of the family came to supper to help us eat a fine hare my father had killed on a hunting trip. When the conversation turned to the fugitive postman, my father abruptly proposed that we change the subject. It was a disgusting business about which he could not calmly express himself. So someone began talking about the probable age of the hare served at the table. My father said it was about a year and a half old. He had guessed this from its pointed nose and ears. My mother added that she had preserved the hare for four days, wrapped up in a cloth soaked in vinegar.

"You can always save some time pounding it with a mallet," said one of the guests.

"Too much danger of breaking the little bones," answered my mother, "and that's mistreating it besides."

Just then our neighbor, who had skinned the hare with great skill, came in, apologizing for being late and bringing the news that someone had caught a glimpse of Nicola the postman on the mountain above the cemetery.

"Just where I shot the hare," exclaimed my father.

"If you had run into him as you chased the hare," someone asked, "what would you have done?"

"I probably would have shot at him," answered my father seriously.

But at a sign from my mother the subject was dropped again. The guests were having their coffee, when a confused and prolonged clucking of the hens came from the garden.

"Go see what's up," said my father. "It must be some stray dog."

At the end of the garden, between the last row of tomato plants and the pine tree by the river, there was a ditch which had once served as a manure deposit. In the ditch, I discovered a man curled up like a terrified beast. He was filthy dirty, had a beard of several days and was trembling all over. With some difficulty, I recognized the postman. He looked at me in supplication.

"Tell your father," he managed to stammer. "Tonight when it's dark, I'll go give myself up to the police. But first I'd like to see a lawyer."

I ran back into the house in a state of panic. I did not know what to say. In my father's presence, while no one else said a word, I mumbled something incoherent. Since it looked as if he were going to run into the garden, I managed to stop him. "It was just a dog," I cried out. "Now he's run away!" My father joked at my lack of courage and, since I was still frightened and trembling, my mother took me off to bed.

After the guests left, my father came to see how I was.

"It wasn't a dog," he said to me.

"No, not a dog."

"Who was it?"

"You can guess."

"Is he still there?"

"In the ditch by the bushes."

"Did he tell you anything?"

"He wants to give himself up to the police as soon as it's dark, and if it's possible he'd like to see a lawyer."

After a pause I added: "Will you beat him up?"

"How can you think that? He's our guest now. He'll be hungry," added my father. "You'll have to take him something to eat and drink. But don't let the neighbors see you."

When the lawyer came, my father did not allow me to be present, but he let me stay in the next room. At first, the former postman's voice was hardly audible and I could not understand what he said. A couple of times I heard the lawyer repeat distinctly: "The right to defense is sacred. Even the worst criminal has the right to defense." The voice of the ex-postman became clearer as soon as he began to explain the cause for his hatred of poor Judith.

"When I brought her the first insured letter," he related, "I asked her for a favor I'd had on my mind a long time. 'Judith,' I said to her, 'I've heard so much about your extraordinary hair. Please let me see it down. It might be fun for you, too.' But she refused right off. 'Before my husband left, I swore to him,' she said, 'that I would never undo my hair in the presence of another man. And I can't commit a sin.' 'This has nothing to do with sin,' I tried to explain. 'Believe me, sin's something else.

The favor I'm asking is entirely innocent.' But no matter how I begged, I couldn't overcome her stubborn innocence. I pretended I was resigned to her refusal, so as not to arouse suspicion. But from that day on I had no peace. Her hair became an obsession with me."

"Do you think that this justifies you before the law?" asked the lawyer.

"It should, shouldn't it?" answered the ex-postman with a voice full of tears. I could hear in his words his bitter disillusionment at the lack of understanding on the part of the man of law. He turned to my father and asked him, "Paolo, what do you think?"

My father took quite a while to answer him. I don't know why, but I was afraid that he would seize the man and throw him down the stairs. But as if to excuse himself, he said: "Nicola, you're here in my house, and you're going to be locked up in prison, where you'll probably spend many years. What can I say to you?"

1965

III

Encounter with a Strange Priest

The Headmaster was a thin prelate, above average in height. To me, at that moment, kneeling beside him, he seemed immense. His hard words came down to me from a great height. "Have you something to say, have you any sort of excuse, any sort of lie, to explain the stupid thing you've done?" he was asking me. "Nothing, Monsignor," I answered, humiliated and resigned. I was holding my head bowed. How much longer was this torment going to continue? I caught sight of a tiny little mouse behind the armchair. I hoped for some diversion, but it vanished under the table. The celluloid collar of my school uniform was pinching my throat, making it almost impossible for me to breathe. "What do you mean nothing?" the angry voice was insisting. "Have you gone stark raving mad?"

On the worn-out red rug, the Headmaster's foot was registering increasing vexation with its nervous tapping. I remember that his feet were long and thin, and clad in fine, soft, slightly worn black shoes with silver buckles. They were all I could see of him. I was at his feet like a beaten dog. "Nothing," I was stammering. "Nothing, nothing at all."

"I'll tell your grandmother," he announced finally in an icy voice. "After what you've done, it's impossible for you to stay in this school, and it's also impossible for me to get another one to take you. There's no doubt of that."

The Headmaster pronounced those words as if they constituted a sentence from which there was no appeal. "There's no doubt of that," he repeated. For my part, all I wanted then was the end of that painful conversation. I could think about the rest of it later. My future was entirely indifferent to me. I just wanted to get up and go away, and not see those feet any more.

"However idiotic you may be," added the Headmaster, who evidently was furious with me for not saying anything, "I don't believe you can expect anything else."

He must have been surprised at my apathy, in strange contrast with my recent rebellion. Maybe he sensed the presence in me of something he could not understand, or perhaps he simply supposed that I did not know how serious my escapade was.

"Yes, certainly, Monsignor," I hastened to agree, just to put an end to my torment. "I really don't expect anything else."

"After everything that's happened," repeated the implacable voice, dissatisfied at my too easy acceptance. "And I'm warning you," he added, "even if your grandmother were to find another school for you, I would feel obliged in conscience to inform your new superiors of the serious mistake you made here. My conscience would not permit me to remain silent."

"Yes, certainly, Monsignor," I hastened to say once more. "Yes, after all that's happened, that's what you'd have to do."

"But, you idiot, if you realize what's happened," he shouted, "why did you do it?"

With this, the elegant silvery shoe rose up and came forcefully down on the old carpet, raising a cloud of dust, which made me sneeze and cough.

This is what had happened. It was 1916, and to complete my secondary studies, for some months I had been placed in a school in Rome under the direction of religious zealots who belonged to a recently founded order. It was hardly a year after the earthquake. I was still in a state of shock from it. The school was in the same neighborhood as the Campo Verano cemetery, the most dreary part of the capital. In those days the vehicles most frequently seen on the streets were hearses. And most of the shops sold ornaments for tombs and things used in funerals.

And some of the inns had very bad reputations. The three-story building was damp, gray and gloomy, with a wide, dusty court-yard which was partly covered by a shed for rainy days, and it was flanked by a church which served the entire neighborhood. It looked like a mission church. The Headmaster of the school was a dignified but brusque prelate, brother of a famous army general. There must have been some family secret to explain why he, too, had not embraced a military career. The preceptor of my dormitory was a more plebeian copy of the Headmaster, with a similar manner of cold severity. He certainly must have suffered grave disappointments in his youth, since he was always in a gloomy mood.

Nor did I find any relief in the company of my fellow students. They were almost all from Rome, and the majority of them were sons of clerks and tradesmen. They were the first city boys I had known, and I did not strike up a friendship with a single one of them. I found them cynical, stupid and noisy, and I frankly did not like them. The difference between my family circle, destroyed in the earthquake, and that cold barracks was insurmountable. But since my natural temperament made me silent and meditative, a condition emphasized by the recent deaths in my family, my not very perceptive superiors considered me the best student, and, what annoyed me very much, set me up as an example to the others.

Now it happened that one day, just before Christmas, without premeditation and with no plausible motive, I ran away from school. I went off without thinking about it, without realizing what I was doing, and with no purpose, simply because at a certain moment I saw the gate in the courtyard wide open. It happened in this way: during recess, a truck loaded with coal came into the courtyard and the driver was slow in shutting the gate. In the brief moment when it was open, I felt myself liter-ally "drawn" to that opening and went out. I wandered around through the unattractive streets of the neighborhood and then headed toward the station. Only when I passed a police station did I realize that I had done something wrong and irreparable, almost a crime. The most inconvenient part of the whole thing was the lack of any explanation. Impossible, therefore, to turn back. Surely my absence, my "flight," had already been noticed. What was I going to tell them? What could I say that would be plausible?

I had very few lire in my pocket and naturally no baggage. I took a room in the attic of a small hotel near the station. I stayed there three days, three interminable days, three days of boredom and anxiety. I did not know what to do, how to use my sudden "freedom." Most of the time I would stand by the window of my little room and watch the trolleys and the wagons go by, and a couple of times I went to the station and sat there for hours, watching the trains come and go. "Well," I thought, "that's life. Now I'm done for." If only I had known why I had done it. The third day, I was "removed" from my room by a policeman and taken back to school. My greatest worry on the way was: "If the Headmaster makes me explain why I ran off, what'll I tell him?" What sort of tale could I invent to make what I had done sound logical or normal? I was frightfully embarrassed, and I hoped that some traffic accident would free me from my problem. I wanted to die. I even recited an Ave Maria to bring on an accident. But the policeman's iron hand led me along.

Naturally there was an enormous scandal in school, the more so since, as I have said, I was considered a model student. When he learned that I had gone, the Headmaster had hesitated to call the police, imagining that I was homesick and had gone home and that I would not delay in writing to ask his forgiveness. But, fortunately for me, as soon as he saw me back and heard from the policeman that I had been found in a little hotel by the station, he did not insist on any kind of report on what wicked things I had done during my three days of absence.

"I don't want to listen to the story of your filth," he yelled at me in a voice altered by anger. And he made me get down on my knees at his feet.

I must confess that this unexpected relief appeared to me to be the result of the prayer I had recited on the way, and I felt once again that I was under the protection of the Virgin Mary. But my silence seemed to confirm what the Headmaster was obviously thinking.

"How was it possible?" he wanted to know.

"I don't know, Monsignor," I answered him. "I just don't know."

"Why didn't you ask your confessor for help, for advice?" he wanted to know. "Or your guardian angel?"

"I don't know, Monsignor," I answered. "I just don't know. Maybe I'll remember the next time."

While waiting for an answer from my grandmother, who, as my guardian, had to decide on my future, the Headmaster allowed me to live in an isolated little room in the school, on the condition that I promise not to tell anyone about the "vile motives" of my escape. No promise was ever so easy for me to give. And, if my schoolmates' imagination was no narrower than the Headmaster's, their criterion of judgment, I must say, was the opposite. And I soon realized that thanks to my undeserved reputation I had grown a great deal in their esteem. My grandmother's answer was not long in coming, and it brought me the news that a certain Don Orione would be willing to take me into one of his schools. Even the Headmaster was happy about the unexpected solution to my problem.

"Would you like to go with Don Orione?" he asked me. "Have you ever heard of him?"

"Oh, yes," I cried with enthusiasm.

To explain my happiness I must relate an episode from the preceding year. It was only a few days after the earthquake. Most of the dead were still lying under the ruins. Help was slow in coming. The terrified survivors lived among the ruined houses in temporary shelters. It was the dead of winter, and that year had been especially cold. New tremors and snowstorms were threatened. The donkeys, mules, cows and sheep had been gathered in makeshift pens, since their barns and stalls had been destroyed. And at night the wolves came, attracted by the strong warm odor of the animals no longer protected by their stables. Night comes quickly in our part of the world, and in that season it's already dark at four o'clock. So it was dangerous to go too far from the shelters. On the mountain, unusually deep in snow, it was impossible for the wolves to get their customary food. Irresistible hunger drove them down into the valley. The smell of the herds in the open air made them bolder than usual, almost mad. To keep them away we had to keep big fires burning all the time. Some nights the cries of these beasts did not let us sleep. Only the light of day brought any peace.

On one of those cold gray mornings, after a sleepless night, I saw a very strange thing happen. A little priest with a ten-day beard, wearing dirty, tattered clothes, was walking among the ruins surrounded by a crowd of children left without parents. The little priest was asking in vain if there was some way of taking the boys to Rome. The railroad had been interrupted by the earthquake, and there was no means of transport for so long a trip. At that moment five or six cars drew up and stopped. It was the King with his suite visiting the devastated towns. As soon as the illustrious people got out of their cars and wandered off, the little priest, without asking anyone's permission, began loading the boys into the cars. The police who had stayed behind to guard the vehicles predictably opposed him. As the priest insisted, there was a violent scuffle which attracted the attention of the sovereign himself. Not in the least intimidated, the priest went forward with his cap in his hand and asked the King to allow him the use of one of the cars for a while so that he could transport the orphans to Rome or at least to the nearest functioning station. Under the circumstances, the King could hardly withhold his consent.

I watched the whole thing, along with some other people, with surprise and admiration. As soon as the little priest had gone off with his carload of boys, I asked the people around me, "Who is that extraordinary man?"

An old woman, who had sent off her grandson with him, answered me: "He's Don Orione, a rather strange priest."

And that was why, a year later, when the Headmaster of the school in which I could no longer remain because of the scandal I had caused told me that Don Orione would take me in one of his institutes, I was very happy. But a doubt suddenly tormented me; had my grandmother told Don Orione why I had to change schools?

In these last few years since his death, a great deal has been said and written about Don Luigi Orione. And much more will be both written and said about his persuasive preaching, his works of charity, about the religious institution he founded which is still flourishing, and about some of his predictions, acts of grace, cures and other exceptional events attributed by the faithful to his intercession with Heaven. But it is not of this that I want to speak, or indeed am able to speak, but rather the unforgettable encounter I had with him as a boy, when he himself was still far from his future renown.

With increasing anxiety I waited in school for the moment when I would see him again. There was nothing left in me of the gloomy desperation of the days of my escape. In church now for the first time I understood the meaning of certain words from the Liturgy: "Prepare thyself, O my soul!"

Don Orione left word that he would be coming to the school to get me and another student from my village (but whose transfer was not for disciplinary reasons). But at the last moment he sent word that he had no time to come. He proposed to meet us in the main room of the station in Rome at a certain hour that same day. This was a great letdown for me. At the agreed-upon time and place, amid the comings and goings and shouts of travelers and porters running to meet the night trains, we found an unknown priest. Not the strange and attractive one I had seen the year before among the ruins of my village, but an ordinary little priest such as can be seen by the thousands in Rome. I was not a little disillusioned, and I immediately showed my contempt for the unfortunate substitute by letting him carry my baggage without lifting a finger to help. After we had taken our seats on the train, the priest explained that he

was to take us to a school in San Remo on the Ligurian Riviera
and that we would therefore be traveling together the whole
night and part of the next morning. This was the first long trip
in my life, but I took no further pleasure in it, since I was
bitterly disappointed at not seeing Don Orione. After a while
the priest asked if I had something to read, and when I said no,
he asked, with the obvious purpose of winning my sympathy, if
I wanted a newspaper and if so which one.

"*Avanti!*" I answered in a dry, obviously provocative tone.

I must explain that at that time I knew the Socialist newspaper only by reputation as an enemy of the Church, tradition
and order. So it would be hard to imagine a more impertinent
request from a schoolboy. Without losing his composure the
priest got off the train and shortly afterward reappeared and
handed me the newspaper. I was amazed and a little mortified,
realizing that in spite of his appearance he was no ordinary
priest, and deserved more respect.

"Why didn't Don Orione come?" I asked him.

My question surprised him. "I'm Don Orione," he told me.
"Excuse me for not introducing myself before."

I was acutely embarrassed at this unexpected news, and felt
contemptible and vile. I immediately put the newspaper away
and stammered excuses for my recent presumption, for having
let him carry the bags, and all the rest. He smiled and confided
that he was happy sometimes to carry bags for impertinent
schoolboys like me. He used an image which I liked enormously
and which moved me. "To carry bags like a donkey," were his
words. And he confessed to me: "My real vocation, a secret
which I want to tell you, would be to live like a real donkey of
God, a real donkey of Divine Providence."

Then I told him that the donkey was the animal I preferred
above all others. "Not the silly donkeys in the public gardens,"
I explained, "but the real ones, the ones the peasants have.
Among other things," I continued, "I find them very smart.
They seem indifferent because they're awfully old, but they
know everything. They're like the peasants who work the

earth," I added, in an attempt to explain what I was getting at.

"Peasants are usually talked about as ignorant people," said Don Orione.

"They know they are hungry, and that's what's important," I said. I had the impression then that I had established a really serious and genuine rapport with him.

The other student with us, who was also coming to San Remo, had fallen asleep. "Aren't you sleepy?" Don Orione asked me. "Oh, no," I assured him. And so we started up a conversation which lasted the whole night, except for some pauses when other travelers came into our compartment. Even though Don Orione was well into his forties and I was a boy of sixteen, I realized that the age difference between us had vanished. He began to talk to me of serious things, not indiscreet or personal ones, but important things of a general nature which adults wrongly do not usually talk about with children. Or if they do, they speak of them in false and didactic terms. But he talked naturally and simply with me in a way I had never seen before; he would ask me to explain certain things, and he got me to answer naturally and simply, without any effort on my part.

Not the least of the extraordinary things about that encounter was the clear and detailed recollection I have of it. At one moment the question arose in my mind that Don Orione might not know the real reason for my change of school, and this uncertainty became intolerable. He recognized the sudden cloud that came over my expression.

"What's the matter?" he asked me. "Are you in a bad mood again?"

"Did you know," I asked him, "that I escaped from school for three days two weeks ago?"

"Yes," he answered. "Your grandmother wrote me and your former Headmaster confirmed it."

"And in spite of that, you'll accept me in one of your schools?" I insisted.

He did not answer right away. "I would like your explanation," he said. "Of course, only if you're able to tell me the truth. Otherwise I'd rather you didn't answer at all, and we can talk about something else."

"What do you mean?" I asked him. "I can't very well promise to be frank with you if I don't know what you mean?"

"Why did you escape from school?"

"I wouldn't have any trouble telling you how it happened," I answered. "But I don't know if you can understand. I don't know if a grown man can understand a boy."

"I'll try very hard," he said. "I was a boy once, too."

So I told him everything that had happened: the open gate, the wandering around to no purpose, the feeling of hopeless guilt, the three days of boredom, anxiety and "freedom." And I concluded, "That's the truth. But I don't know if you can understand me. I don't know if a grown man can understand a boy."

He smiled, nodding his head, and seemed to be filled with compassion.

"Yes, certainly," he said. "I can understand."

At the Civitavecchia Station some travelers entered our compartment. They were coming from Sardinia. They were tired, and they stretched out to sleep. After one of them turned out the light, leaving only a weak blue emergency light, Don Orione's features began to look like those of the priest I had seen the year before in my village. I reminded him of the royal cars and told him why I had hardly recognized him a little earlier.

"I believe you," he told me. "That day I must have looked like a bandit."

"And a kidnaper to boot!" I added, laughing, in an effort to match his way of expressing himself.

He told me about the troubles he had had those days, and about several of the villages which had been destroyed in the earthquake. Every day the disaster had seemed bigger than the way it had been described in the beginning. The snow and wolves made communication with the villages in the mountains difficult; and every delay in helping the wounded, whose cries could be heard in the ruins, the sick who were without shelter and the wandering children, increased the number of victims. It had taken him twenty-seven days to cover the area, and that month he had never gone to bed and never had a full night's rest, but only an hour or two on improvised couches, not daring to take off his shoes for fear of freezing his feet. As soon as he had gathered together a certain number of orphans or abandoned children, he would take them to Rome, and then return immediately to the scene of the disaster to try to save others.

"Everyone has the strength he needs, as we priests often say."

"The sheep has his, and the donkey his," I said, unable to hide my admiration.

"Physical strength is a curious thing," he added. "Just think that when I was your age, I was sent home from a Franciscan cloister because my health seemed weak and ill-adapted to the monastic life."

The masthead of *Avanti!* was still protruding from the pocket of my jacket. I apologized for requesting that particular newspaper and explained why I had. I had heard that it was the newspaper of the poor. Most of my friends back home were very poor. "How sad," I said, among other things, "to see your intelligent schoolmates denied more education just because they're poor, and forced, instead, into a life of humiliation and hardship."

Then Don Orione began to tell me how hard his own humble origins had been. His father belonged to one of the lowest and most miserable categories of workers, the street pavers, and he as a boy had often had to help in that unrewarding trade. Then a little later, when he had been accepted by the diocesan seminary, to pay for his board and room he had had to work in the cathedral. He told me several amusing and often moving stories about his difficult adolescence. Among them he recalled one about his first trip to Rome, for which he was provided with only a loaf of homemade bread and five lire.

To hear him talk like this gave me great pleasure, a kind of new peace and serenity. (I decided then that the next day I would make notes on every word we had exchanged.) The train was proceeding up the Tyrrhenian coast. In the darkness of the night, I could hear the sound of the ocean, which was new to me. I seemed to be on my way to discovering the world.

"Aren't you tired?" Don Orione asked me at one point. "Don't you want to try to sleep?"

"I wish this trip would never end," I stammered. What made the most lasting impression on me was the peaceful tenderness of his glance. The light of his eyes had the goodness and clear-sightedness which are sometimes found in certain old peasant women, in certain grandmothers, who have patiently endured all kinds of trouble and who therefore know and can guess at the most secret sufferings. At times I had the impression that he saw me more clearly than I saw myself, but this was not an unpleasant impression. A couple of times he interrupted the conversation, as if to interject a parenthesis.

"Remember this," he said to me. "God is not just in church. In times to come you will have moments of desperation. Even if you think that you are alone and abandoned, you won't be. Don't forget that."

He said this with the same voice and the same simplicity with which he said everything else. But I could see that his eyes were shining with tears. At La Spezia we found the station filled with girls in Red Cross uniforms, and with sailors and soldiers of every rank. For Italy this was the second year of the First World War. A bloody offensive was in progress on the Austrian front. We heard that they were waiting in the station for a trainload of those who had been seriously wounded.

"How long will this horror last?" I said. Don Orione made no comment, but the exclamation did not escape him. Dawn came over the Levantine Riviera, along with a violent thunderstorm. Don Orione read his breviary for half an hour, then was absorbed in his thoughts for a while.

"I would like to tell you a secret about the war," he said, almost in a whisper. "Yesterday was an especially important day for me. I was received by the Pope in a private audience. Some weeks ago I wrote a letter to the Holy Father about the conduct of Christians in relation to the war, and he summoned me to talk about it. I'll read you the rough draft of my letter."

I was very moved. "Why does he want to talk about these things to me?" I asked myself. After looking in his suitcase, he brought out some papers covered with writing.

"When the head of a congregation is received by the Pope in a private audience," he continued, "especially if their conversation is about the Church's religious and moral authority, he has no right to repeat what was said. But this time I really believe I can make an exception."

Slowly, so that I would understand it well, Don Orione read me the draft of the letter he had sent to the Pope. (This letter has not been published, but it must certainly be among his papers.) It was in a vehement and beautifully impassioned style resembling the writings of Saint Catherine of Siena. It was a letter humble and bold at the same time, suggesting the audacious idea of a Christian initiative on the part of the people to go over the heads of the recalcitrant governments and put an end to the war. Therefore the Pope had summoned Don Orione and greeted him affectionately, but he pointed out that his plan would not work, since the Church could not appeal to the people and the soldiers to do anything but pray. Naturally, like an obedient son, Don Orione had accepted what the Pope told him, as he put it, in words of profound sadness. And he realized that Christianity's place in modern society was more tragic and contradictory than he had thought when he wrote the letter. (I don't know if Don Orione could foresee then the deep and lasting impression his words would make on me. I think he did; otherwise his little talk would have had no point.)

At Genoa we had to change trains and wait for two hours for the coach to Ventimiglia. It was raining hard, but Don Orione insisted on showing me at least part of the city, which was familiar to him but which I did not yet know.

"You won't often get a guide like me," he said.

"But you must be tired," I objected. "Because of me you haven't closed your eyes all night, and you know the city already. And it's no fun to walk in the rain without an umbrella."

"After a certain age," he explained with a smile, "you have very few pleasures, only reflections of them. Fathers take joy from the pleasures of their sons."

So I had to follow him. We left the other student in the waiting room of the station to watch over our baggage and went off into the city. He showed me the monument to Columbus, some ancient palaces, the façade of a church and the port facilities. We walked fast, close to the walls, under the roof gutters to keep out of the rain as best we could. He was in front and I was behind; he would warn me in advance when a gutter was broken and we had to jump away from the wall to avoid a soaking.

We came to a doorway and stopped for a minute to catch our breath. Then Don Orione remembered that he still had some post cards in his pockets to mail. He had intended to mail them from Rome, but he said he had forgotten to. I was a little surprised at the great number of picture post cards, all written out and stamped, which Don Orione began to take out of his pockets. Even when I thought there could not be any more, he continued to take them out of pockets whose existence I had not dreamed of. It was pure comedy.

"There are about three hundred of them," he explained. "They're Christmas greetings from me to the members of a boys' club I founded at Tortona. The boys are all workmen's sons, and for some of them this will be their only Christmas card."

"The thing to do," I suggested, thinking of the train schedule, "would be to run to the central post office and mail them all at once."

Don Orione did not accept my suggestion for a rather curious reason.

"It would not be a good idea to mail them all at once," he explained. "If we did that, the cards would all be stamped by the same clerk on their way out, and distributed by the same postman when they arrive. You would run the risk that they might lose patience with so many of the same cards and throw some of them out. It would be better to divide up the cards among several different mailboxes, so as to separate them right from the beginning."

I was amused by this clever trick of a man expert in the ways of the world. Coming back to the station, we divided up the cards and set out on opposite sides of the street in a contest to see who could finish first. I had the advantage of my age, since I could run, push people aside, ask for directions, and even make quick side trips into nearby streets, without attracting attention. But Don Orione finished his distribution before I had finished mine. On the train he asked me if I had mailed all the cards, every last one of them, and I had to confess that I had held one back for myself.

"So that I'll have a Christmas card, too."

"But that card is for someone else," he pointed out. "It's not for you, even if you take it. You've been a rather bad postman."

At the next stop, Oneglia, I got off to mail the last card. The long trip was coming to an end. When, at the approach to San Remo, Don Orione explained that he would introduce us to the Headmaster of the school and that he would have to leave that very evening, I was heartsick, and tried to hide it. "That's what life is like," I was thinking. "As soon as you come to like someone, you lose him."

We came to San Remo about noon; the sun shone brilliantly and for me it was an entirely new sight of an unforgettable splendor. Every object stood out sharply in the crystalline light. The countryside was more attractive than I had thought it would be, and for the state of mind I was in it was almost too lovely. For the first time I was seeing gardens with palm trees, wide beds of carnations, avenues lined with mimosa, tangerine and lemon trees. And my thoughts turned to my village, where the poor who had escaped from their ruined huts were living in the mud, in caves and in barracks, and had to keep fires burning at night to frighten the wolves away. I began to feel an entirely new pain taking shape in the depths of my being.

That evening, when Don Orione was to leave, I heard that he had sent someone to find me to say good-bye. But I hid. I did not want him to see me cry. I lay in the dark thinking about what had happened. I knew that I would understand it better with the passage of the years. A few days later, Christmas morning, I got my first letter from Don Orione, an affectionate, extraordinary letter twelve pages long.

"I've been waiting for answers to urgent administrative questions and haven't got them!" burst out the Headmaster as he handed me the letter. "But to you he writes half a book!"

"Yes, he's a very strange man," I had to agree.

1949

IV

Polikushka

After the earthquake, the headquarters of the Farmers' League had been re-established in a hut belonging to the county. But it was almost deserted because most of the active members had been drafted on account of the war. The hut was surrounded by donkey stables and pigsties, in the dirtiest part of the village. Three or four old farmers met there every Sunday night, mainly to give the impression, especially to themselves, that the Farmers' League was still in operation. Depending on the season, they would sit just outside or indoors around a table, exchanging a word or two, or smoking a pipe, in the dark because there were no lights. At that hour the other farmers were usually at the inns. The three or four League members, understandably, would rather have been at an inn with glasses of wine in their hands, but the authorities had already tried to take the hut away on the ground that it was not used, so they had to show that it was. "We need it for our meetings," they had declared.

To give up their "headquarters" would mean the end of the League. One day or another the war would have to end, and they could not let the young demobilized farmers find it gone just when they would need it most. One day or another, of course, was just a manner of speaking. The women went to church to pray for peace, but the men knew that impatience with fate never did any good.

Within the hut were some relics which had been found after the earthquake among the ruins of the old headquarters. Hanging on a wall was a picture representing Christ the Redeemer, wearing long red overalls with a banner above Him that read, "Blessed are they which do hunger and thirst after righteousness." Under the picture, hanging from a nail, was the trumpet that had once been used to call together the members, since many of them could not read and thus could not be summoned by posters. All in all, the use of the trumpet was an expeditious and pleasant way of getting people together. But with posters it would have been easy to explain in advance why the meeting was being called. With the trumpet this was impossible. And so it happened that every time its blast was heard echoing through the streets of the village, an understandable anxiety would arise. This happened at night, when the farmers were coming back from the fields, and it was understood that the meeting was to take place right away. In the families of the landowners and other rich, well-born people this uncertainty took the form of apprehension if not downright fear. What's happening? Another meeting? But what do they want? Are they mad? Then mothers would lean out of windows and balconies and call home their children in loud voices, as a brood hen calls her chicks, so they would not get involved in any trouble.

There was no one to call me any more, and perhaps for that reason I felt strangely attracted to those poor people who, worn out by their day's labors, came at the summons of the trumpet. And so I became involved in their meetings, which were held in the courtyard of an old Franciscan convent which in its day had been founded by another poor man, St. Francis of Assisi. Even though they were the same people I saw on other occasions, in town, at church, or at the market, these sudden gatherings made a profound impression on me. My heart would beat violently. There was always some stranger at those meetings who would talk in a loud voice, but I could not understand much of what he was saying. All my attention was focused on the people, who seemed to me transfixed.

Usually no one paid any attention to me. But one night something unpleasant happened.

"What're you doing here?" a farmer asked me in a threatening voice. I looked at him without breathing, as if I had been caught doing something wrong. "Are you going to plow a furrow, too?" he insisted with growing anger.

"No," I answered, forcing a smile on my face to placate him. "Right now I'm in school." And I showed him some books I was carrying.

An older man I knew by sight came to my rescue and put his hand on my shoulder as a sign that I was under his protection. I stayed next to him until the end of the meeting, and then I walked with him to his home, which was in the new part of the village that had grown up among the vineyards.

"What's your name?" I asked him.

"Lazzaro," he answered. Then he added, "When I was a young man, I was very close to your father."

"Why did that man want to kick me out of the meeting?"

"Maybe on account of your books."

"What?" I exclaimed. "Is there anything wrong with studying?"

"No, there's nothing wrong with it, but there are some educated people who use their education to take advantage of the poor. Didn't you hear what was said at the meeting?"

I admitted that I had not. Then he tried to explain it to me. For several years, there had been a special law which exempted farmers in the southern part of Italy from certain petty taxes. The farmers in our region, however, did not know about this law and therefore continued to pay them. Why hadn't anyone told us? Without a doubt the clerks in the tax collector's office knew about it, as well as the town clerks, the lawyers, the schoolteachers and the priests—in short, all the educated people who read the papers. Why had they hidden it from us? This news seemed unbelievable to me.

"How can it be possible?" I asked. "Lazzaro, tell me what you think. Why hasn't anyone said anything about it?"

He hesitated to answer me, perhaps to avoid saying unpleasant things about people I knew. But I insisted.

"Lazzaro, why won't you tell me? Do you think the truth should be kept from boys, too?"

But some other people came up just then, and we could not continue our conversation.

From that meeting grew my friendship with Lazzaro. I liked him; he did not have much to say; he was rough, modest and without a trace of obsequiousness or fear. He had not had much education and he could barely read and write, but he knew a side of life of which I was entirely ignorant. For example, on the origins of the war then going on, and of all wars, Lazzaro's knowledge was simple and sure. Wars, he explained, are a remedy governments use to keep down the ever-increasing number of farmers. And for the same purpose they send cholera and other epidemics to the poor people.

"But don't the rich die, too?" I countered.

"Yes, they do, and that's God's vengeance," he explained. "Of course, governments have no interest in exterminating the people who work the earth. Otherwise who'd do that work? And what would the gentlemen eat? And that's why wars last only so long. During the fighting the Red Cross keeps a constant control of the number of victims. And at a certain point it says, 'O.K. That's enough for now.' "

Of course, these were paradoxical opinions which did not convince me in every detail, but that an honest and reasonable man like Lazzaro would give them out as his own was cause enough for bitter pain and torment for me.

My visits to the League to meet Lazzaro were not unobserved, and they soon became cause for scandal among those who knew me, since I was still a student, and because my family, without being rich, was considered above the farmer class. I did not do much in the League, except to write some protests to the authorities on its behalf; sometimes even to the government in Rome on problems which Lazzaro explained clearly to me, and which I had to rewrite several times before I arrived at something satisfactory.

One day one of my classmates took me aside to tell me, "Do you know that they've started saying that you're a Red?"

"Nonsense," I answered. "I've never been to the dye-works." But I told Lazzaro about it when I next saw him.

"There're people who say I'm a Red, too."

As often happened Lazzaro did not answer right away.

"I haven't the least feeling of having changed my skin," I added.

"As for color," Lazzaro finally answered, "it seems to me that a man's like water. If you take a glass of water, you see right away that it has no color. But a lot of water, a great river or the sea, easily takes on a coloration."

"Because of the sky?" I asked.

"Because of the sky," he confirmed. "In the same way each of us alone is like a glass of water. Where does the color come from?"

"From the mass?" I asked.

"Not from the mass," he explained. "A mass of sheep is still a mass of sheep. And there are hardly three or four of us."

"From what then?" I insisted.

"Whenever we get together, He promised to be with us," Lazzaro explained, pointing to the picture of Christ in the red overalls.

By the way he expressed himself, and everything else, Lazzaro was what is called a good Christian. For many years he had been a Prior of the Confraternity of Saint Francis. But he had not set foot in church since the priests had used the church bells to disrupt the farmers' meetings. The first time it happened, it was a great surprise for the people who filled the square. Given the hour, no one could explain the unexpected ringing. It was late for Vespers and early for the Ave Maria. Even less explicable was the fact that all the church bells were going full blast as if the Resurrection had come. The foreigner who was talking about the new agricultural contracts, standing on a table at one side of the square, was inundated by the wave of sound which came from the nearby church and paused, waiting for it to stop. It did stop, only to be unleashed again as soon as the man started talking once more. The murmuring in the square took on a threatening tone; but Lazzaro, by standing with open arms at the threshold of the church, prevented the crowd from invading it. From that day he had stayed away from church, particularly since the same thing happened again in the same circumstances.

"Why don't you go to church?" the parish priest asked Lazzaro one day. "Don't you hear the bells? You used to come regularly."

"Yes, I once thought those bells were the voice of God," Lazzaro answered him. "But now you've made them the voice of the landowners. May God forgive you."

Hearing these words, some other farmers who were about to enter the church withdrew and went away.

One evening, I made my usual appearance at the League. Seeing some schoolbooks under my arm, Lazzaro suggested, "Why don't you try to read us something from those printed pages?"

"Sure," I answered, "I'll pick out something good."

And since the next day was a holiday, we made a date for that evening. The idea of reading excited me a lot, and I was surprised that I had not thought of it on my own. But as soon as I started thinking of what text to choose, I was rather embarrassed. My education had been entirely scholastic, and we no longer lived in a period when Dante's *Divine Comedy* could be read in public in the squares of Tuscany. Even less suitable seemed the nonscholastic books I then had, most of them D'Annunzio. To take one of those in hand seemed far worse than reading in Latin, with which the farmers had some contact through the Liturgy. But I had to keep my word, and I had to push myself not to fail in the important undertaking.

At one point I remembered the words of a poor doctor who practiced in a village in our county. He was known as an anarchist; he led a very difficult life and was therefore treated with mistrust and contempt by the respectable families.

"I have a book I could lend you," he had once said to me.

The next day I went to his house to ask for his help and advice. In the summer sun, on a road covered with blinding dust, it was not a pleasant trip. I found the doctor in his squalid kitchen, fixing something to eat.

"Will you have a bite with me?" he asked.

I excused myself. "I have a date," I said.

While he talked, he broke up some bread, put it on a plate and poured bean soup over it from a pan. I explained my problem to him.

"Read to the peasants?" he asked. "I don't know what to tell you to read them."

"They're simple, but they're not stupid," I insisted.

"I know them and I know it's hard," he countered. "Come on," he said suddenly, going into the next room which served as his study.

The room did not show much respect for hygiene. Books, medicine samples, sanitary objects and clothes were scattered everywhere in a state of confusion, even on the chairs and floor.

"Try this," he said, handing me a dog-eared little book. "If it's successful, I'll give you another one."

It was a collection of stories by Tolstoy.

On the way back I thought of resting a while under a tree at the edge of a meadow, to get out of the great heat, and to have a look at those stories. I knew that Tolstoy was known as a great writer, but I had never read anything of his. When I began reading, I forgot about time and appetite. I was deeply affected. I was stirred most of all by the story of Polikushka, which describes the tragic end of a servant whom everyone had held in contempt because of his drinking and pilfering. Hoping to rehabilitate himself by doing an important job for his mistress, he lost the money entrusted to him and hanged himself in desperation. The writer who could portray a servant's suffering with such sincerity must have been a very good and brave man. The sad, slow pace of the story revealed a compassion beyond the usual pity of the man who is moved by his neighbor's troubles, and averts his glance so that he will not suffer, too. Divine compassion must be like this, I thought, the compassion which does not relieve a creature of his pain, yet on the other hand does not abandon him but helps him to the end, without ever revealing itself. It was incomprehensible, even absurd, to me that I had come to know a story like that only by chance. Why didn't they read it in school?

I read the whole story over again that afternoon, finding new beauties which I had missed in the first reading. I was sure that my little audience would like it, in spite of some difficulties with the Russian names, especially the nicknames—and I thought of ways to get around them.

But when I arrived at the League building, I got the impression that the old men had forgotten all about our agreement. They were sitting on the doorstep, and one of them was reciting the long-drawn-out account of his encounter with a priest. I showed Lazzaro the book I had in my hand.

"Let's be quiet and listen to the book," he suggested.

"We're not kids any more," grumbled one of them. "Fairy tales are for kids."

"But there are stories for grownups, too," I protested. "Just be patient and listen."

"What's it about?" one of them wanted to know. "Can't you tell us what happens?"

"It's a story about a man like you, who was born in Russia," I answered, losing patience. "I thought you'd like the story of a poor man."

It looked as if they were tolerating it more for my sake than out of real curiosity.

I began reading in a confident voice, but after the first few sentences I realized that the minute description of the overseer Igor Mikhailovich visiting his master, the notation of every detail of his behavior, and the examination of his most deeply hidden thoughts formed a skein whose thread my listeners had probably already lost. My voice faltered, and I raised my eyes from the page to look at Lazzaro.

"Do you follow?" I asked.

"Couldn't you tell us in two or three words what happens?" repeated one of the old men.

"If that were possible, the author would have written just two or three words and nothing else," I tried to explain.

"Read on," Lazzaro encouraged me.

Then it occurred to me that this was not a text to be read aloud. The doctor who had lent it to me was right. Give up? Impossible! But since I had already read it twice alone, I tried to proceed with my eyes skimming the text, summarizing or skipping whatever seemed like a digression.

I lingered a little over the description of the drawing of lots for military service in the little community of Pokrovskoye, and again over the portrait of Polikushka, a good man who after every drunken binge, and every time he was caught pilfering, promised to mend his ways, a man who had practiced a little of every trade in his life—stable boy, weaver, brick maker, and even veterinarian—though he knew next to nothing about any of them.

"In other words, he was a real crook," one of the old men interrupted, "someone to lock up in jail and forget about."

I felt my voice fading. If they had not the least sympathy for poor Polikushka, what good was it to read the story?

"Go on," Lazzaro told me.

I put the book aside and told them the end in a few words: about Polikushka's trip to the city on his mistress' confidential errand, the withdrawal of the money from the rich merchant, the loss of the precious hoard, finally his desperation, his vain search and his suicide.

"They didn't find the money?" Lazzaro asked me.

"It was found and brought back to the lady to whom it belonged. But she was so shocked at seeing Polikushka hanged that she refused to accept it."

"How did the story end?" one of the old men asked me.

"What?"

"That money. You said there was a lot of it."

"The lady left it to the man who found it, named Dutlov."

"Didn't she give it to the servant's widow?"

"No. Not to the widow."

I said that I was tired and left them.

I didn't know what to think of what had happened, or rather I did not want to think about it. That evening while I was doing the homework that had piled up in the last few days, I was told that someone in the street wanted to see me. It was a farmer who belonged to the League but who was not very active.

"No one told me," he complained. "If I had known, I would have come. What's the story about the man who hangs himself and then they find the money he lost?"

"I'll tell you about it some other time," I promised him, "but I'm busy now."

In the years that followed I was too emotionally involved in other things to have much time to read literary works. The only books I used were histories and economic tracts, but not even these were for educational purposes; rather were they for immediate practical use, to write little newspaper articles, in which the rashness of my judgment was equaled only by my sincerity. I was reminded of Polikushka just once, during a visit to Moscow. One night, around the Pushkin Monument, when I was with some leaders of the Soviet Young Communist League, I saw two soldiers hauling a drunken farmer away by the scruff of the neck. I recognized him at once.

"Couldn't you get him released?" I asked my friends.

"Why?" one of them answered. "He's nothing but a parasitic insect!"

1965

V

Emergency Exit

Non vi si pensa, quanto sangue costa.
(They think not how great the cost of blood . . .)
—DANTE, *Paradiso,* XXIX, 91

1.

That evening in November, 1926, just after the promulga-
tion of the "special laws," some of us had escaped arrest by
fleeing to a little villa on the outskirts of Milan which had been
rented some time before by one of our comrades who was dis-
guised as a painter. In the working-class neighborhoods the
streets were deserted, the bars closed and silent and the houses
dark. This gave the city a gloomy atmosphere in that cold,
damp season. The police, in full battle dress, were carrying out
unannounced raids in that area of the city, surrounding sus-
pected houses as if they were enemy fortifications under siege.
The number of those arrested was already quite high and was
added to day by day from the names and addresses which the
police picked up in the raids, from the reports of spies and
agents provocateurs, and from the testimony of the weakest of
those arrested, who were unable to stand up under threats or
torture.

In other cities and provinces much the same thing was happening on a large scale. The newspapers that were still allowed
to be published (those in open opposition were already being

suppressed) had been told not to mention the arrests, but to report instead the praises of the Italian dictatorship which, to our shame and mortification, were being sung by eminent representatives of democracy and liberalism in other countries. But the bulletins of the three or four party messengers who gathered information in the principal regions and brought it to the underground headquarters left no doubt about the intention of the dictatorship to exterminate every trace of resistance. The Communists were the only ones who had an underground organization of any efficiency, but in some provinces the police raids had already destroyed our communications network. And there were many comrades who, having escaped arrest, were asking for semipermanent refuge in a city other than their own, as well as false documents so they could travel and find themselves new "occupations."

Those of us who had already been living under false names and professions for a long time, hiding our conspiratorial activities under innocent and conventional appearances, were certainly in a more advantageous position. But we were none too safe either, since possible betrayal or weakness on the part of any of those arrested could give the police information leading to us. Thus I had been warned that evening not to go home, since my house appeared to be under police surveillance. Together with others who found themselves in the same predicament, I sought a temporary refuge in the house of our friend the pretended painter. Having put a man on guard nearby, and after agreeing on what to do in case of emergency, we resigned ourselves to passing the night on chairs, since the house was rather sparsely furnished and had only one bed.

Along with the bogus painter and his wife, we were a bogus Spanish tourist, a bogus dentist, a bogus architect and a German girl who was masquerading as a student. We had all known each other for two years, but our relations up to that day had consisted exclusively of technical collaboration in various branches of the illegal organization. We had not yet had the time or opportunity to become friends. At the most, some of us knew the home towns and family situations of the others, through the inevitable reflections these facts cast on the complicated expedients of life outside the law. Why, then, has that evening's chance encounter remained impressed for so long on my memory?

The dentist happened to say at a certain moment: "This afternoon I passed by La Scala. There was a long line of people waiting to buy tickets for the next performance. I stopped a while to look at them, and I had a strong impression of being in a group of madmen."

"Why madmen?" asked the Spanish tourist. "Is opera an insanity to you?"

"Not normally," admitted the dentist. "But how can you be amused by music in times like these? You'd have to be really crazy."

"Art is not merely amusement," observed the Spanish tourist.

"If the music-crazy people could see us now and know who we were and what we were doing," added the painter, "they would almost certainly think we were crazy. It's not easy to know who the really crazy people are. Perhaps it's one of the hardest of all things to determine."

The dentist did not like the turn the conversation was taking.

"You can't risk your life and freedom the way we're doing," he replied sharply, "and then reason calmly like someone who is *above the struggle.*"

"You can throw yourself into the struggle," answered the painter, "you can hit and kick your opponent, but you don't necessarily have to butt him with your head. Isn't it better to save your head for some other purpose?"

"Isn't our struggle an ideological one?" asked the Spanish tourist. "Isn't your head committed?"

"My head is committed, certainly, but not my eyes," explained the painter with a smile. "In other words," he added, "I'd like to continue seeing things with my own eyes."

"I don't understand," stated the dentist. "The risk you're running by staying with us seems to me way out of proportion to your small degree of commitment. How about explaining yourself?"

There was a pause of embarrassed silence. The conversation at that point could have ended badly. Through the window we could see three trucks loaded with soldiers passing by. The lady of the house closed the shutters and served us coffee.

"In our time, all roads lead to Communism," said the Spanish tourist to restore peace among us. "We can't all be Communists in the same way."

"I've bet my life on the proletarian revolution," said the painter. "If I haven't bet my eyes as well, it's only to reserve for myself the right to see what's happening to my life. But all life is a bet. In the same way, to explain it a little better, one of my best school friends became a nun, thus betting her life on Paradise. I mean the celestial Paradise, not to be confused with the workers' paradise. I can assure you that I'll keep my bet. Why shouldn't I? No one has the right to doubt my honor!"

"But the proletarian revolution is not a game of chance!" chided the dentist.

"Yes, I know that," said the painter. "I know that winning my bet doesn't depend on chance, but on the skill and strength of the players and all the other things we read about in the manuals of the party schools. And that's why I participate not only as a bettor, but as a player as well, as a player entirely absorbed in the game and who has wagered himself. All of himself, I repeat, except his eyes."

"I don't understand," said the dentist.

"In short, I refuse to wear a blindfold," concluded the painter. "I'll do everything I'm required to, but with my eyes open."

"Fine," said the Spanish tourist, "but I don't understand whether your bet is more important to you than other things—say, war, exploring the South Pole, taking care of lepers, white slavery, counterfeit money?"

"Why not?" the other answered, laughing. "But it's likely that even in each of those possible professions, I would have tried to keep my eyes open, tried to understand."

"One's born a Communist," said the German girl.

"But one becomes a man," commented the painter.

"Now," said the dentist, "can you tell us how you ended up betting on Communism?"

"That would be a long story," he answered seriously. "And some things, frankly, you just wouldn't understand."

"Tell us your long, incomprehensible story," said the German girl. "We'll drink coffee and stay up listening to you. Even if we don't understand, it won't matter. The most beautiful stories aren't always understandable."

"And will you tell your stories?" the painter asked us in a challenging tone.

"Yes," the dentist agreed. "We'll drink coffee and listen."

"Let's think a minute," warned the painter. "It may be dangerous to look back. It may be dangerous for any of us, including myself, while we're in the midst of the struggle, to examine the how and the why, to look back. At a certain moment the die is cast and *rien ne va plus*—if you're on the floor, you have to dance."

"But can you separate the struggle from the motives which led you to take part in it?" asked the Spanish tourist. "Do you think it's dangerous to recall the motives which led us to Communism?"

"It's a long night," said the German girl. "Let's tell each other our incomprehensible stories. We'll drink coffee and stay up."

So we passed the night trying to explain to each other how and why we became Communists. The explanations were anything but exhaustive, but by morning we had all become friends. "Yes, it's true," we said to each other as we separated, "that you can come to Communism from every direction."

(The next year the pretended dentist was arrested and tortured. He refused to betray his collaborators and died in jail. The bogus painter continued to do his political duty until the fall of Fascism. After the liberation he retired to private life. I never heard anything more about the German girl.)

In the ensuing years, I have often thought back on the confidences we shared at that meeting—especially when the need to understand, to realize, to compare the meaning of the action in which I was involved with the initial motives for that involvement, took entire possession of me and left me no peace. And if my literary work has any meaning, in the last analysis it is this: at a certain moment writing meant for me the absolute necessity of bearing witness, the urgent need to free myself from an obsession, to affirm the meaning and define the limits of a difficult but permanent break, and of a more sincere faith.

For me writing has not and cannot be, except in a few rare moments of inspiration, a serene aesthetic pleasure. Rather it has been the painful and solitary continuation of a struggle, after separation from my good friends in the party. And the difficulties I sometimes find in expressing myself certainly do not derive from disobeying the rules for writing well, but from a conscience which labors to heal certain hidden, perhaps incurable wounds and which obstinately continues to insist on its own integrity. To be truthful it is evidently not enough merely to be sincere. It is therefore not without effort that I have set out to tell this story without recourse to parables.

2.

At the founding Congress of the Italian Communist Party, at Leghorn in 1921, I brought with me the adherence of a great part of the Socialist youth with whom I had been associated since 1918. From the time of the war, the political orientation of Italian Socialist youth had been so decidedly critical of reformist Social Democracy that this fact caused no great surprise. But it is not easy to describe what the political orientation of that majority was; the very expression "political orientation" is an exaggeration, since the psychological traits involved were more crucial. We were simply in revolt against everything and everyone. What purified and refined the infantile and neurotic elements of our rebellion was the enormous flame of hope lit by the Russian Revolution.

That November evening in Milan, I wanted to explain to my

friends why I had chosen the Zimmerwald variety of Socialism at the age of eighteen, when a war was going on and I was still a schoolboy. To do so, I had to go back step by step in my memory to my early adolescence and even to events in my childhood to find the earliest origins of my revolt, which, when it later assumed political form, was to find such extreme expression. This is not boasting. At eighteen, and in wartime, one does not enter a revolutionary movement that is persecuted by the government, for trivial or opportunistic reasons. But the devil take facile psychological explanations. It is better to try to reconstruct a life's journey from the outside.

I was born and grew up in a rural area in the Abruzzi, at a time when what impressed me most, as soon as I reached the age of reason, was the grating, incomprehensible, almost absurd contrast between private family life—which at least appeared decent and honest—and social relations, which were very often hostile and deceitful. About the misery and desperation of the southern provinces of Italy numerous episodes are now known (I have told some of them myself). I do not refer to historically important events but to everyday little banalities in which the strange two-faced behavior of the people among whom I grew up expressed itself. And every once in a while really ugly things happened which shocked those who were not used to them.

I was still a boy when, one Sunday as I was crossing the square with my mother, I witnessed the stupid and cruel spectacle of a local young man of good family sicking his dog on a little seamstress as she came out of church. The poor woman was thrown to the ground, badly hurt, and her clothes were ripped to shreds. There was indignation throughout the village, but discreet indignation. No one ever understood where the poor woman got the unfortunate idea of suing the young man, since it had the predictable result of adding the farce of official justice to what she had already gone through. She had the sympathy of everyone, as I have said, and was secretly helped by many; but she could find no one who would testify before the judge, nor a lawyer who would take her case. But the young man's lawyer (considered to be of the left) and some bribed witnesses perjured themselves, swearing to a grotesque version of the incident, accusing the woman of having provoked the dog. The judge, a worthy and honest man in private life, acquitted the young man and ordered the poor woman to pay the costs of the trial.

"I did it with great regret," the judge excused himself some months later at our house. "On my honor, believe me it was most distasteful. But if as a private citizen I myself had been present at the disgusting spectacle and could not have avoided condemning him, still as a judge I could only consider the evidence produced at the trial. And unfortunately, as you know, this was favorable to the dog. "A real judge," this honest official loved to pontificate, "must silence his personal feelings and be impartial."

"Of course," my mother used to say, "but what a horrible profession. It's better to mind your own business at home. Son," she said to me, "when you grow up, be anything you want, but don't be a judge."

It was repeated to us on every occasion that minding one's own business was the fundamental condition of honest and peaceful living. This was confirmed by the teaching of the Church. The virtue recommended applied exclusively to private and family life. But from my earliest years I liked to hang around the streets, and the friends I preferred were the sons of poor farmers. My tendency not to mind my own business and my spontaneous friendships with the poorest of my contemporaries were to have disastrous consequences for me. My most vivid memories of childhood and adolescence are of this kind.

There are other exemplary episodes like that of the dog of good family and the seamstress engraved on my memory. But I would not like to raise a doubt, with stories like these, that the sublime concepts of justice and truth were unknown or held in contempt. Oh, no, not at all. They were often discussed in school, in church and on public occasions with great eloquence and veneration—but in rather abstract terms. The better to characterize this strange and curious situation, I should add that it rested on a deception of which everyone, even the children, were aware. And yet it lasted, since it was based on something more than the ignorance and stupidity of the people.

I recall in this connection an animated argument which arose one day in the catechism class between us boys and the parish priest. It was about a puppet show which we had all seen the day before. It concerned, as I still remember well, the dramatic adventures of a boy pursued by the Devil. At one point the puppet boy appeared on the stage trembling with fear and, in flight from the Devil, hid under a bed in a corner of the stage. Soon thereafter the Devil puppet came on.

He looked in vain for the boy.

"But he must be here," said the Devil puppet. "I can smell him. Now I'll ask these good people in the audience." And he turned to us and asked: "My dear children, have you perhaps seen the bad boy I'm looking for anywhere around here?"

"No! No!" we all answered with the greatest possible energy.

"Where is he then? Why can't I see him?" insisted the Devil.

"He's left. He's gone away," we answered. "He's gone to Lisbon." (In our common speech and in our proverbs to this day, Lisbon marks the farthest limit of the globe.)

I should explain that since none of us had foreseen that we would be questioned by a Devil puppet when we went to the show, our behavior was entirely spontaneous and instinctive. And I suppose that in any other country in the world children would probably have reacted in the same way. But to our astonishment our priest, an educated and pious person, was not entirely pleased. He explained this with regret in the little chapel of Santa Cecilia, where he usually gave us our catechism lessons. We liked the place because the Roman martyr painted above the altar had the beautiful features of a blond girl, distracted and melancholy, holding in her arms an object which bore a curious resemblance to a domestic utensil called the *chitarra* which was used in our homes to make spaghetti. The picture so attracted us that to rescue us from its seductiveness, at least during catechism time, the priest was obliged to turn our benches around so that our backs were to Santa Cecilia.

"Your behavior during the puppet show was a great disappointment to me," he told us after we had sat down.

He was worried. We had told a lie, he said. For a good end, of course, but it was still a lie. We should never tell lies.

"Not even to the Devil?" we asked in astonishment.

"A lie is always a sin," answered the priest.

"Even before a judge?" asked one of the boys.

The priest looked at us sternly.

"I'm here to teach you Christian doctrine and not to talk nonsense," he said. "What goes on outside the Church does not concern me."

And he returned to his explanations about truth and lies in general, using beautiful and difficult words. But we were not interested in the question of lies in general. We wanted to know, "Should we have told the Devil where the boy was hidden, yes or no?"

"That's not the point," the poor priest repeated to us in an effort to solve this thorny question. "Lying is always a sin. It can be a big sin, a medium-sized one, an in-between one or a little one. But it's still a sin."

"The truth is," we said, "that the Devil was on one side and the boy on the other. We wanted to help the boy. That's the truth."

"But you told a lie," repeated the priest. "To a good end, I realize, but it was still a lie."

To put an end to all this, I raised an objection of unheard-of perfidy and, in view of my age, considerable precocity.

"What should we have told the Devil if it had been a priest instead of a boy?" I asked him.

The priest blushed and avoided answering my question, and, as punishment for my impertinence, made me remain on my knees in front of him for the rest of the lesson.

"Have you repented?" he asked me at the end of the lesson.

"Of course," I answered. "If the Devil asks me for your address, I'll certainly give it to him."

It was certainly unusual that the discussion had taken this turn in a catechism class, but in the family circle and generally in private among adults an open-minded attitude was quite common. However, a lively mind did not really disturb the humiliating and primitive stagnation of the community's social life. It merely made it harder to bear. Everything was arranged so as to teach children to submit and to mind their own business.

3.

Some time before, democracy had introduced a new technical detail—the secret ballot—into the relationship between the State and the citizen which, although not enough by itself to change things, every once in a while produced surprising and scandalous results. Though these were isolated episodes with no lasting consequences, they caused concern since they revealed what was smoldering under the ashes.

I was seven years old when the first political campaign of which I have any memory took place in my part of the world. At that time political parties did not exist where we lived, and so the announcement of the campaign did not attract much attention. But everyone was very excited when the news got out that one of the candidates would be none other than the Prince. There was no need to give his full name to know which Prince was meant. He was the owner of the great estate which had been created by the usurpation of the lands reclaimed in the preceding century by the draining of Lake Fucino. About eight thousand families (that is, the majority of the local population) were engaged in cultivating the thirty-five-thousand-acre estate. The Prince therefore was deigning to ask for the vote of "his" families so that he could become their Deputy in Parliament. His agents, who brought the news, accompanied it with a little talk, delivered in the liberal intonation of the times. "Of course no one is obliged to vote for the Prince," they would say, "that goes without saying, just as no one can force the Prince to hire anyone to cultivate his lands who votes against him. This is the era of true liberty for all: you are free, and so is the Prince."

The enunciation of these ideas about liberty produced an understandable alarm among the farmers, since, as can well be imagined, the Prince was the most hated person in our region. As long as he stayed on the invisible Olympus of large land-owners (none of his eight thousand tenants had ever seen him, not even from a distance) hatred of him was publicly admissible. It was like cursing unpropitious gods. It did no good, but it provided some relief. But now the clouds were about to burst open, and the Prince was to descend to the level of mortal man. For this reason any expression of hatred against him had to be confined henceforth to the restricted circle of private life, and preparations had to be made to greet him in the streets with all the appropriate honors.

My father was one of the few who seemed uneasy at this logic. He was the youngest of a group of brothers who were peasant-proprietors, the most youthful, the most restless, and the only one with any proclivity to insubordination. One evening his brothers came to urge him, in the common interests, to be prudent and careful. For me this was a very instructive evening. (No one paid any attention to me, because adults think that children don't understand such things.) After serving the men something to drink, the women retired into the next room. I was curled up in a corner by the large fireplace, around which the men were seated in a semicircle. They were tall, strong and solemn, the oldest wearing long beards, and they all had huge feet and powerful knees, shoulders and hands. In spite of age and comfortable family circumstances, they continued to do the hard labor themselves; they drove the wagons, they guided the plows and supervised the threshing. The need to work seemed a physical necessity for them. They were churchgoing men, but not clerical; they respected law and order, but did not kowtow to the authorities. They had been raised to show courage in the face of danger, a maddened beast, a flood or a fire. That evening, however, they looked simply embarrassed.

"The Prince's candidacy is just a big joke," admitted the oldest. "Political candidacies should be reserved to lawyers and other windbags. But since the Prince is a candidate, there's nothing we can do but support him."

"If the Prince's candidacy is just a big joke," argued my father, "I don't understand why we have to support it."

"Because, as you know, we work for him part of the time," they told him.

"But not in politics," said my father. "In politics, we're free."

"We don't cultivate politics, we cultivate the land," they answered. "Not all our land is on the hills. Since we also work land from Lake Fucino, we work for the Prince."

"But our contract says nothing about elections. It concerns potatoes and beets. As voters, we're free."

"Well, the Prince's managers are also free not to renew our contract," they reminded him. "That's why we have to come out for him."

"I can't vote for someone just because I'm forced to," said my father. "I'd be ashamed."

"No one will know how you vote," they said. "In the privacy of the voting booth you vote as you like, freely. But during the campaign we must all come out for the Prince."

"I'd be glad to do it if I weren't ashamed," said my father. "But, believe me, I'd just be too ashamed."

To settle the issue, my uncles and my father reached this compromise: he would come out neither for nor against the Prince.

The Prince's campaign trip was carefully prepared by the civil authorities, the local police, the national police and his own estate administrators. And finally one Sunday the Prince deigned to pass through the principal towns of the constituency, without making any speeches and without even stopping. His trip was long remembered in our district, chiefly because he made it in an automobile and this was the first time that new vehicle had been seen there. The very word "automobile" had not yet entered into our local dialect. Instead, the farmers called it a "horseless carriage." There were strange legends about the invisible motive force which took the place of horses, about the diabolical speed of the new vehicle, and about the ruinous effects, especially on the vines, of the smell it left behind. That Sunday the whole town turned out to see the Prince on the main street, where he was supposed to pass by. Numerous signs of admiration for him were visible. Triumphal arches had been erected, and the crowd in its Sunday best showed an understandable excitement. The "horseless carriage" arrived late and roared through the town without stopping, without even slowing down, leaving a thick white cloud of dust behind. Later, the Prince's agents explained to whoever cared to listen that the "horseless carriage" ran on "gasoline vapor" and could not stop until it ran out of gasoline. "It's not like with horses," they said. "With horses, all you have to do is pull the reins; but there are no reins to pull. Did you see any reins?"

Two days later, a curious little old man arrived in the square from Rome. He was wearing glasses and carried a little suitcase and a black stick. No one knew him; his name was Scellingo. He said he was an oculist and that he was running on the People's Party ticket against the Prince. A curious crowd surrounded him, most of them children and women, who could not vote. I was among the children, in my short pants and with my schoolbooks under my arm. We asked the little old man to give us a speech. He was no orator and so he limited himself to saying, "Tell your fathers that the vote is secret. Nothing more." Then he added: "I'm poor, I make my living as a doctor, but if any one of you has something wrong with his eyes, I'll cure him for nothing." We brought him an old woman who sold fruit and who had had something wrong with her eyes for many years. He cleansed them and gave her an eye dropper with some medicine and told her how to use it. Then he said to us (we were just a group of children), "Remind your fathers that the vote is secret." Then he left.

But the election of the Prince was so certain, to judge from the festive crowds which had greeted him on his lightning tour, that the authorities and the Prince's agents announced in advance a celebration of the inevitable victory. My father, true to the agreement with his brothers, abstained from supporting either candidate and was strangely silent. But he succeeded in having himself included among the examiners of the results. Great was the astonishment of all when it was announced that in the privacy of the ballot box an overwhelming majority of the voters had chosen the unknown oculist. It was a huge scandal. The authorities called it a despicable betrayal. And, what was worse, it was of such proportions that the Prince's agents could not take reprisals against individual farmers. (As a consolation the Prince was appointed Senator by the King.)

After that, life went back to normal. No one asked himself, "Why can't the will of the people show itself except sporadically?" No one went that far. And yet it would be incorrect to conclude that what held them back was fear. The people were neither cowardly nor lazy. The rigors of the climate, the ruggedness of the work and the harsh struggle for existence had made them hardy and tenacious. But centuries of resignation, the consequence of violence and deception, weighed them down. Experience seemed to justify the blackest pessimism. These wounded and humiliated souls were capable of going through the worst torments without complaining, until they broke out in unexpected revolts. It was not for nothing that in my home town, which then had a population of about five thousand, order was kept by twenty policemen under the command of a lieutenant. . . .

4.

There was no love lost between the soldiers and the police during the First World War, since the police were stationed behind the lines, and some of them, it was said, paid too much attention to the wives and fiancées of the absent military men. In small towns these rumors are almost always given very precise personal references. And so one evening it happened that three soldiers who had come back from the front on a short leave had an altercation with some policemen and were arrested. This step, ridiculous and hardly chivalrous in itself, was made monstrous by the police commandant's decision to cancel the men's leaves and send them back to the front. Since I was a good friend of one of them—who was later killed in the war—his mother came in tears to tell me of this injustice. The mayor, the judge and the parish priest, whom I asked to intervene, all said it was beyond their power to help.

After I had been left alone, I had moved to the poorest and least respectable part of town, which consisted of one-story huts lacking even basic hygienic facilities. To get there you had to pass a ditch which the authorities called the Tagliamento, after the river which then formed the front line between the Italian and Austrian armies. In other words, this neighborhood was enemy territory. The inhabitants liked this strange nickname, and they soon took measures appropriate to a war zone. First they created a blackout by smashing the street lamps with stones. In this way it became dangerous for even the police to approach the Tagliamento at night. Anyone so unfortunate as to come there was greeted by a volley of stones from unknown assailants.

The evening the three soldiers were arrested, when the news spread among the huts that they were to be sent back to the front the next day, we young people decided this was an injustice that should be prevented. In other words, we felt we should attempt another "revolution."

In our dialect, which was extremely short on political terminology, we used this fatal word even in referring to a simple demonstration without the permission of the authorities. In that time of war, for example, there had already been two "revolutions," the first against the town council because of bread rationing, the second against the Church because of the transfer of the bishop's see to another town. The third, which I am about to describe, went down in history as the "revolution of the three soldiers."

Since the soldiers were to be escorted to the train at five o'clock in the afternoon, the "revolution" was scheduled for half an hour earlier, in front of the police barracks where they were confined. Unfortunately, this had consequences more serious than we had bargained for. It began as a joke, since we needed only a few people to set it in motion: one to climb the church tower at the appointed time and ring the bells with a hammer, as is done in case of fire or other public danger; a second to blow the trumpet of the Farmers' League; and the rest of us to meet the farmers coming back from the fields to tell them what was happening and persuade them to come to the barracks.

In a few minutes a noisy and threatening crowd composed of women, boys and old men (since the young ones were at the front) had gathered before the police barracks. The demonstration soon progressed from shouts to stone-throwing, which the police gathered in the barracks courtyard answered with volleys fired into the air. This firing excited the crowd all the more. The siege of the barracks lasted until late. Their fury had made the peasants unrecognizable. Finally the windows and doors of the barracks were broken; the police, under cover of darkness, fled through the orchards and fields; and the soldiers, whom by now everyone had forgotten, went home unobserved. And so we boys were left absolute masters of the place.

It was a memorable night. We gathered at the top of the hill which overlooked the barracks. It was rocky and bare, with great holes and thistle bushes, yellow broom and wild roses, a territory with which our games had made us familiar. It was a clear and solemn night, with a breeze that brought us the smells of wild herbs from the mountain. When we counted heads, we discovered that one of our number had been wounded in the arm by a rifle bullet. But instead of thinking at once that he should see a doctor, we looked upon him with envy. "How did you do it?" we asked him. He was flattered and smiled, but he did not answer, as if it were a secret. Meanwhile, at the foot of the hill, the agitation seemed to have spent itself; the streets were deserted, though every once in a while a mother would lean out of a window to call the children who had not come home, imploring them to come in with affectionate family nicknames.

"Mothers are really silly," apologized one of our group who had been called.

"They make us look ridiculous," added another.

On me the mountain breeze had another effect, however, conveying a less romantic view of the situation and of my responsibilities. The others realized my unease.

"What'll we do now?" they wanted to know. (My authority derived more than anything else from the fact that I had studied Latin.)

"Tomorrow morning," I said, "the town is sure to be occupied by hundreds and hundreds of armed men, police of all kinds, who will come from Avezzano, Sulmona, Aquila, and maybe even from Rome."

"But before they get here, what'll we do tonight?" the other boys wanted to know.

"A single night is hardly enough to set up a new order," I said, trying to guess what they wanted.

"Couldn't we take advantage of the fact that everyone's asleep to establish Socialism?" some of the others proposed. They had only recently heard that word for the first time, without knowing what it meant; and perhaps they thought anything was possible.

"I don't think," I had to answer, "I really don't think that one night would be enough to establish Socialism."

"One night might be enough to sleep in our own beds before we go to jail," one finally suggested.

And since we were tired, we found that advice both timely and appropriate.

Such violent episodes, with the inevitable consequences of mass arrests, trials, exorbitant legal costs and jail sentences, reinforced the mistrust, suspicion and resignation in the minds of the farmers, as is easy to understand. The State reacquired its identity as the Devil's own creation. A good Christian, if he would save his soul, should avoid contact with it as much as possible. The State always stands for theft, corruption and special privilege. It can be nothing else. Neither law nor force can change that. If calamity sometimes strikes it, it is the judgment of God alone.

5.

In 1915 a violent earthquake destroyed a good part of our province and in thirty seconds killed thirty thousand people. What surprised me most was to see with what matter-of-factness the people accepted this tremendous catastrophe. In an area like ours, in which so many injustices went unpunished, the frequency of earthquakes seemed so plausible a fact that it required no explanation. On the contrary, the surprising thing was that earthquakes did not occur more frequently. In an earthquake, everyone dies: rich and poor, learned and illiterate, authorities and people. An earthquake accomplishes what words and laws promise and never achieve: the equality of all. An ephemeral equality, for when fear had died down, collective misfortune became the opportunity for even greater injustices.

What happened afterward was therefore no surprise, and that was the reconstruction by the State. Because of the way it was done, because of the intrigue, fraud, embezzlement, favoritism,

scheming and thievery of every sort to which it gave rise, it
appeared a far greater calamity than the natural cataclysm.
From that event dates the origin of the popular belief that if
humanity is bound to get thoroughly skinned some time or
other, it will be not in time of earthquake or war, but in a
postwar or post-earthquake period.

A friend of mine, who had been fired from one of the government offices in charge of the reconstruction, one day gave me
some precise data which proved that crimes had been committed by engineers who had been his colleagues. Quite disturbed, I hurried to consult with some persons in authority
whom I knew to be upright and honest men, to ask them to
denounce these crimes. Not only did the gentlemen I consulted
not contest the authenticity of the proofs; they were in a position to confirm it. But they advised me against "getting involved in the affair," and they added affectionately: "You have
to finish your education, you have to make a career for yourself.
You shouldn't compromise yourself with things that don't concern you."

"With pleasure," I answered. "Certainly it would be better if
the report didn't come from a boy of seventeen, but from adults
in respectable positions."

"We are not madmen," they replied in indignation. "We
mean to mind our own business and nothing else."

I then talked with some "reverend" clergymen, as well as
some of my more courageous relatives, and all of them, revealing their greater or lesser familiarity with these crimes, im-
plored me not to get mixed up in such a hornet's nest, to think
of my education, my career and my future.

"With pleasure," I would answer, "but are any of you willing
to report the thieves?"

"We're not crazy," they responded, scandalized. "These matters don't concern us."

I then began to wonder seriously whether it might not be
appropriate to make a new "revolution" with some other boy,
which would end with a fire in the government offices. But the

friend who had given me the documentation on the crooked dealings dissuaded me, in order not to destroy the very proof of the crimes. He was older and more experienced than I, and he suggested that I get the denunciation printed in some newspaper. But which one? "There is one," my friend explained, "which might be interested in giving space to such a report, and that's the Socialist paper." And that was how I came to write three articles (the first ones in my life) to describe and explain in detail the corruption of the government engineers in my part of the world. I sent them to *Avanti!* The first two articles were printed at once and caused an uproar among the readers, but no reaction from the authorities. The third article did not appear, as I was to learn later, because a prominent Socialist lawyer intervened with the editorial board. In this way I learned that the system of deception and fraud oppressing us was vaster than I had imagined and had invisible ramifications that extended even to the Socialists. The partial denunciation, coming as a surprise, contained enough material for several trials, or at least for a parliamentary board of inquiry. But nothing happened. The engineers whom I had denounced as thieves and accused of specific charges made no attempt to justify themselves or even to issue a denial. After a brief interval, everyone went back to minding his own business.

The student who had dared to make this challenge was considered by the more charitably-disposed to be impulsive and strange. It must be borne in mind that the economic poverty of Italy's southern provinces offered few possibilities for advancement to the young men who came out of school by the thousand every year. Our greatest industry then was government employment. It did not require exceptional intellectual qualities, but it did demand a docile character and political conformity. The young men from the south, who had grown up in an impoverished atmosphere, if they had the least pride or human sensitivity, tended naturally to anarchy and revolt. Taking a government job therefore meant a renunciation, a surrender and a mortification of the soul for those who were still on the threshold of their youth. For this reason it used to be said, "Anarchists at twenty, conservatives at thirty"—and this was the true foundation of society in southern Italy.

The education one got in the schools, whether public or private, was not designed to strengthen character. The situation has changed from the time of my adolescence, but I do not know if it has improved. For most of grade school and high school I attended private Catholic institutions. The humanistic instruction was moderately good; the training in private personal habits was tidy but ingenuous; but the civic education was dreadful, in part because of the open conflict between Church and State. For example, the Church's teaching of history was explicitly hostile to the official version; the mythology of Italy's *Risorgimento* and its heroes—Mazzini, Garibaldi, Vittorio Emanuele II and Cavour—were objects of scorn and contempt. The then fashionable literature—that of Carducci, Pascoli and D'Annunzio—was despised. And in one sense, this teaching offered certain advantages, since it developed the student's critical capacity. But these same ecclesiastical teachers, since they had to prepare us for the State school examinations, and since the reputation and prosperity of their institutions depended on our showing, also taught, and recommended to us for the examinations, points of view which went counter to their own convictions. On the other hand, the examiners from the State institutions, knowing that we came from Church schools, took delight in quizzing us on the most controversial topics, and ironically praised the lack of prejudice in the instruction we had received. The falsity, hypocrisy and two-faced character of this expediency were too shameless not to be very disturbing to anyone with a love of culture. But it was inevitable that the unfortunate average pupil ended up considering his diploma and future job as life's supreme goal. In school all my prayers ended with one request: "Oh, God, help me to live without betraying myself."

"Those born around here are really unfortunate," Dr. F.J., from a nearby village, used to repeat to me. "There's no third course; either you rebel or you play the game." He had rebelled. He declared himself an anarchist. He gave Tolstoyan speeches to the poor. He became the scandal of the whole area. Hated by the rich, scoffed at by the poor, and with the secret sympathy of only a few, he finally lost his job as municipal doctor and literally died of starvation. His end served as an example for the respectable families. "If you don't come to your senses," said the mothers to their sons, "you'll end up like that madman."

6.

The journey I have been tracing is too summary not to seem forced. I can guarantee its sincerity, not its objectivity. Recalling that period with my contemporaries, I was sometimes astonished that they had little or no memory of events which had such a decisive influence on me; while they, on the other hand, had vivid recollections of other circumstances which to me were pointless and meaningless. Are these, my contemporaries, all unwitting accomplices? Certainly not. And by what decree of fate, or through what inner strength or neurosis, does one decide at a certain age to be a "rebel"? Do we choose or are we chosen? Where do some people get their spontaneous intolerance of submission on the part of others, their total incapacity to let injustice go by—even if it only affects others? And that sudden feeling of guilt when they seat themselves at a groaning table when others do not have enough to eat? And that pride which makes persecution preferable to contempt?

Perhaps no one knows. There's a point at which even the fullest confession becomes a mere statement or description, not an answer. Everyone who has reflected seriously about himself and others knows that some decisions are secret and certain vocations mysterious and unaccountable. In my rebellion there was a point at which love coincided with refusal to cooperate. Both the facts which justified my indignation and the moral reasons which made that indignation necessary were given me by the place where I grew up. The step from submission to subversion was very short; all I had to do was apply to society the principles that were considered valid for private life. And that is how I explain the fact that everything that I may have written up to now, and probably everything I will write in the future, even though I have traveled and lived abroad for many years, refers only to that part of the country which can be seen from the house where I was born—no more than twenty or thirty miles in any direction.

It is a countryside, like the rest of the Abruzzi, lacking in political history and with an almost completely medieval Christian background. It has no monuments of note other than churches and monasteries. For many centuries its only illustrious sons were saints and stonecutters. The conditions of human existence there have always been particularly difficult. Pain has always been considered the first of natural calamities; and the Cross in that sense is shouldered with honor. For people with any vitality the most accessible forms of rebellion against fate have always been to join either the Franciscan order or the anarchist movement. Under the ashes of skepticism the ancient hope for the Kingdom, the ancient expectation that love will take the place of law, the ancient dreams of Gioacchino da Fiore, the Spirituals and the Celestines have never died out among those who suffer most. And this is a fact of enormous and fundamental importance which no one has considered sufficiently. In an exhausted and tired area such as ours, this has always seemed to me a real resource, a miraculous reserve. The politicians are unaware of it, the clergy fear it. Perhaps only the saints are able to sense it and to make use of it. But it has always been much more difficult, if not impossible, for us to see the ways and means to a political revolution, *hic et nunc,* to the creation of a free and healthy society.

I think I arrived at this discovery after I moved to the city and had my first contact with the workers' movement. It was a sort of flight, an emergency exit from an insupportable solitude. It was the cry of "Land! Land!"—the discovery of a new continent. But it was not easy to reconcile my state of mental rebellion against an old and unacceptable social order with the "scientific" requirements of a minutely codified political doctrine; I realized that belonging to the party of proletarian revolution was not to be confused with membership in just any political party. For me as for many others, it was a conversion, a complete commitment, which implied a certain way of thinking and a certain way of living. Those were times when calling oneself a Socialist or a Communist meant risking everything, breaking with one's relatives and friends and not being able to find work. The material consequences were therefore serious, and the difficulties in readjusting one's thinking were no less painful. The private little world within, the "Middle Ages" which I had inherited and which were rooted in my soul and from which in the last analysis I had derived the initial impulse toward revolt, was shaken to its foundations as if by an earthquake. In the privacy of one's conscience everything came up for discussion and everything turned into a problem. It was at the moment of the break that I felt how tied to Christ I was in every fiber of my being. And for this reason I tolerated no mental reservations. The little devotional lamp I kept burning before the tabernacle of those institutions that had been most dear to me was extinguished by an icy wind. The terms "death," "love," "good," "evil" and "truth" changed their meanings or lost meaning entirely. However, the dangers seemed easier to challenge since I was no longer acting alone. But who can describe the private dismay of an underfed, provincial youth living in a squalid bedroom in the city, when he has given up forever his belief in the individual immortality of the soul? It was too serious a thing to discuss with anyone; my friends in the party would probably have found it something to deride, and I had no other friends. And so, unknown to anyone, the world changed its whole appearance for me.

7.

The conditions of life imposed by the Fascist coup were very hard on the Communists. But these conditions also served to test some favorite Communist theories, and gave the party the opportunity of fashioning a type of organization in no way incompatible with Communist mentality. So I, too, for some years adapted myself to living like a foreigner in my own country. I had to change my name, give up every previous family tie and habit, settle in provinces where I had never lived before, and lead a life which betrayed no external sign of conspiratorial action. The party became family, school, church and barracks. Outside of it the rest of the world was to be entirely destroyed. The psychological mechanism by which the individual Communist gradually identifies with the collective organism is now well known. It is the same phenomenon that occurs in certain religious orders and military schools. Every sacrifice was willingly made as a necessary personal contribution to the "price of collective redemption." It should be clearly understood that the ties which bound us to the party were stronger, not in spite of the dangers and sacrifices they exacted, but because of them. This also explains the attraction of Communism for some types of young people and women, for intellectuals, and for people who are more sensitive and more inclined to generosity and who suffer most from the "wastefulness" of bourgeois society. And those today who think they can lure the best and most serious of the young people from Communism with games of billiards in well-heated pool halls take a very limited and rather cynical view of human nature (though the quality of membership in a mass party is obviously different from that in a small underground one).

It is therefore little wonder that the first political crises in the Communist International left me rather indifferent. They sprang from the fact that the principal parties in the new International were anything but homogeneous even after they had accepted the famous twenty-one conditions for admission dictated by Lenin. They shared an aversion for "imperialistic war" and its results, and a critical view of the reformist ideas of the Second International, but otherwise, for better or worse, they reflected the unequal stages of development of the various countries. That is why there were notable differences of opinion between Russian Bolshevism, which took shape in a political environment absolutely without freedom and a social life with little differentiation, and the leftist Socialist groups from the Western countries. The history of the Communist International was therefore a story of intrigues and aggressive moves by the controlling Russian group against every independent expression on the part of the other affiliated parties. One after another, these parties were obliged to break with the Communist International: those groups most tied to parliamentary traditions (Frossard) ; those most respectful of law and most outraged by any slightly adventurous "putsch" (Paul Levi) ; the libertarian elements who had lost their illusions about Soviet democracy (Roland-Holst) ; the revolutionary union leaders who were opposed to bureaucratic submission to the Communist Party unions (Pierre Monatte, Andrés Nin) ; those who were most opposed to ending the collaboration with the Social Democratic masses (Brandler, Bringolf, Tasca) ; and the far left, which could not stand some of the opportunistic moves of the party (Bordiga, Ruth Fischer, Boris Souvarine) .

These internal crises originated and developed in a sphere far from the one in which many of us were operating, and for this reason we were not much involved. I do not take any credit for this now—on the contrary, I am merely trying to explain it. The growing degeneration of the Communist International, which was becoming more tyrannical and bureaucratic, both repelled and disgusted me, but there were other strong reasons which postponed the break: loyalty to party friends who had been killed or imprisoned, the lack of other organized anti-Fascist forces in Italy, the rapid political and in some cases moral decadence of some of those who had already left the Communist

Party, and finally the illusion that an improvement of the International could be brought about by the Western proletariat if there was an internal crisis in the Soviet regime.

Between 1921 and 1927 I had various opportunities to go to Moscow to participate in meetings and congresses as a member of Italian Communist delegations. What most struck me about the Russian Communists, even in truly exceptional personalities like Lenin and Trotsky, was an absolute incapacity to discuss with fairness any opinions contrary to their own. The dissident, just because he dared to contradict, was nothing but an opportunist, a traitor who had sold out. The Russian Communists could not conceive of a loyal opposition. What a "reckless aberration" it is for polemicists who call themselves materialists and rationalists to affirm in absolute terms the primacy of morality over intelligence! It has already been justly observed that to find a similar folly, one would have to go back to the heresy trails of the past.

When I left Moscow in 1922, Alexandra Kollontaj told me jokingly, "If you should read in the papers that Lenin has had me arrested for stealing the Kremlin's silverware, it will mean simply that I have not been in full agreement with him on some problem of agricultural or industrial policy." Kollontaj had acquired her sense of irony in the West, and she used it only in conversation with Westerners. But even then, in the exciting years when the new regime was being created and when the new orthodoxy had not yet taken over all cultural life, how hard it was even for us Western Communists to reach an understanding with Russian Communists on the simplest and most obvious of problems! How difficult it was, not merely to agree but simply to understand each other, when talking about what freedom meant for a man in the West, even a worker.

I remember one day I tried for hours to explain to one of the directors of the State Publishing House why she should be ashamed of the intimidating atmosphere to which Soviet writers were subjected. She could not understand what I was trying to say.

"Freedom is the possibility of doubting," I had to explain, "the possibility of making a mistake, the possibility of trying, of experimenting, of saying no to any authority, literary, artistic, philosophical, religious, social or political."

"But that would be counterrevolutionary," murmured the eminent functionary of Soviet cultural life. Then she added, just to get back at me, "We're happy not to have your 'freedom.' But we have our sanatoriums instead."

When I observed to her that the expression "instead" had no meaning, "since freedom is not merchandise to be sold," and that I had already seen sanatoriums in other countries, she laughed in my face.

"Today you feel like making fun of me," she said. And I was so completely moved by her candor that I did not dare to contradict her. There is no worse slavery than the one of which you are unaware.

It was very exciting to see the enthusiasm of the Russian youth in those first years when a new world which everyone hoped was more humane than the old one was being created. And how bitter was the disillusionment when the political democracy that had been promised at the beginning did not materialize, although with the passing of the years the new regime grew stronger, its economy prospered and armed attacks from abroad came to an end. On the contrary, the dictatorship became all the more repressive.

One of my best friends, the head of the Russian Communist Youth, Lazar Schatzky, confided to me one evening how sad he was that he had been born too late to participate in either the 1905 Revolution or the one of 1917.

"But there will be other revolutions," I answered him. "There'll always be need of revolutions, even in Russia." We were in Red Square, not far from Lenin's Tomb.

"What kind of revolutions," he wanted to know, "and when can we expect them?"

Then I pointed to the tomb, which was still a wooden one then. Every day we could see long, interminable processions of poor farmers in rags passing by.

"I suppose you respect Lenin," I said. "I knew him, too, and I have a strong memory of him. But you must admit that this superstitious cult of his mummified body is an offense to his memory and a disgrace to a revolutionary city like Moscow."

In short, I proposed to get a can of gasoline and to celebrate a "little revolution" on our own, by burning up the totem tomb. To be frank, I did not think that he would accept my proposal, but I thought he would at least laugh and that he would understand what I meant by "There'll always be need of revolutions." But my poor friend was horrified in the extreme and began trembling. Then he begged me not to repeat such an awful thing, not to him and especially not to anyone else. (Ten years later, sought as an accomplice of Zinoviev, he committed suicide by throwing himself from the fifth floor of his apartment building.) What tricks memory plays! I have been to numerous huge parades of people and armies in Red Square, but what I remember about it better than anything else are the emotion and frightened voice of my young friend who came to so tragic an end. It might also be said that that memory is more meaningful "historically."

8.

One of the few people to whom I dared to speak openly was Anatoly Lunacharsky who held the position of Commissar of Education and Culture in Moscow from the time the new State was established. I became close to him after our first meeting, when he was assigned to translate into Russian a little lecture I gave in a Moscow theater. Lunacharsky had an excellent command of Italian, and it was always a great pleasure to talk with him, not only because of his knowledge of Italian language and

Italian culture, but also because his mind had been developed abroad, outside the closed circle surrounding Lenin. This manifested itself, among other ways, in a cordial and tolerant conversational tone of an almost Western style.

"Don't make us scapegoats for our entire history," he said to me one day when I was complaining about the narrow-mindedness of his bureaucrats. "We are behind you in more than just technical things. Through the proletarian revolution we must achieve not only the industrial revolution accomplished in the West by the bourgeoisie, but we must also bring about the spiritual progress so lacking here. We have never had a Machiavelli, a Galileo, a Giordano Bruno, a Beccaria, to mention only the Italians. And to have men like them it is clearly not enough simply to translate their writings into Russian."

"I still don't understand why the Comintern sends people who still have so much to learn to Italy to give us instructions," I ventured.

"That's Grigory Zinoviev's job," Lunacharsky interrupted, and changed the subject.

It will not be easy to write the history of the Communist International, and no doubt it would be premature to do so now. How is one to separate the banal from the essential in the interminable discussions at its congresses and conventions? Which pages should be abandoned to the mice in the archives, and which should be recommended to intelligent people in search of understanding? I do not know. What my memory insistently offers me may perhaps seem only strange to some, and I have no trouble admitting that feeling does not always coincide with historical judgment. One day, in a special commission of the Comintern, we were discussing the ultimatum from the central committee of the English trade unions ordering its locals not to join the minority movement directed by the Communists, on pain of expulsion. After the representative of the British Communist Party had presented the seriousness of the dilemma—since if the ultimatum were accepted, there was a risk that the minority movement would be dissolved, and if it were refused, the movement might leave the trade union organization—the Russian delegate Piatnisky proposed a solution which seemed as obvious as Columbus' egg.

"The locals should state that they submit to the order, and then in practice do the exact opposite," he suggested.

The British Communist interrupted: "But that would be a lie."

This naïve objection was greeted with a burst of laughter, frank, warm, interminable laughter the like of which the gloomy offices of the Communist International had certainly never heard, laughter which rapidly spread all over Moscow, since the Englishman's incredibly funny answer was immediately telephoned to Stalin and the most important offices of the State, leaving new waves of astonishment and hilarity in its wake, as we learned later. "In judging a regime it is very important to know what it finds amusing," said Togliatti, who was with me.

As I have said, I have made only a few trips to Moscow, and they were limited to my duties as a member of the Italian Communist delegation. I have never been part of the Communist International apparatus, but I could follow its rapid corruption by observing the transformation of an occasional friend who belonged to it. One of these, a typical case, was the Frenchman Jacques Doriot. I met him for the first time in Moscow in 1921, when he was still a modest, sincere, eager and sentimental young worker. As far as I could see, it was his obvious docility and willingness that had gotten him chosen for the international organization in preference to other young French Communists more intelligent and better educated, but also more individualistic. He fulfilled every expectation. From year to year, he rose in rank among the officers of international Communism. And from year to year, whenever I saw him, I watched him change for the worse, always more skeptical, cynical and unscrupulous, and in his political view of men and the State, ever more Fascist. If I could overcome what I suppose is an understandable repugnance, and write a true biography of Jacques Doriot, I would develop this theme: "How one becomes a Fascist in the Communist movement." I met Doriot in Moscow in 1927 on the very day of his return from a political mission in China. To me and some of his friends he gave a disturbing account of the mistakes of the Communist International and the Russian Government in the Far East. But the next day, before the Executive in plenary session, he affirmed the opposite with great emphasis. We listened to him in astonishment. "It was an act of political wisdom," he confided to us after the meeting, with the little smile of the superior man.

His case is worth mentioning because it is anything but isolated. The internal vicissitudes of French Communism later took Jacques Doriot out of the Communist International and gave him the chance to reveal himself as the adventurer he had become. But many others, no different from him in private, have remained at the helm of Communist parties. Togliatti alluded to the double dealing and demoralization within the circles of the Communist International and to the atmosphere of intrigue within the central offices at the end of his speech before the Sixth Congress of the International when he asked permission to repeat the words of the dying Goethe: "Light, more light!"

Beyond the internal contradictions deriving from its own heterogeneous character, the Communist International felt instantly repercussions from every difficulty within the Soviet State. After the death of Lenin, it appeared clear that the State was not going to escape what seems to be the fate of every dictatorship: the gradual restriction of the influence of those who participate in the direction and control of political power. The Russian Communist Party, which had suppressed all rival parties and abolished every opportunity for general political discussion in the Soviet assemblies, itself fell under an extraordinary regime. The political goals of its members were soon replaced by those of the apparatus. From that moment every difference of opinion among the leaders was destined to end up with the physical extinction of the minority. The revolution which had laid its enemies low began to devour its favorite sons. The thirsty gods allowed no truce. Marx's optimistic phrase about the natural decay of the Socialist State was revealed to be a pious illusion.

9.

In May, 1927, with Togliatti I participated as a representative of the Italian Communist Party in an extraordinary session of the enlarged Executive of the Comintern. Togliatti came from Paris, where he was in charge of the party, and I came from Italy, where I was directing its underground apparatus. We met in Berlin and continued our journey together to Moscow. The meeting had been called, ostensibly, to discuss the directives to be given to Communist Parties in the struggle "against the imminent imperialist war," but its actual purpose, as was soon apparent, was to begin the liquidation of Trotsky and Zinoviev, who were still members of the Comintern Executive. In order to avoid surprises, the plenary sessions were preceded and prepared for in every detail by the so-called "senior convent," consisting as usual of the heads of the most important delegations. Togliatti insisted that I accompany him to those restricted sessions, to which only he from the Italian delegation would ordinarily be admitted. But in view of the complications which were about to arise he preferred to have the support of a representative of the underground organization.

At the first meeting we attended we had the impression that we had come too late. It was held in a small office of the Comintern, and the German Ernst Thälmann was presiding. He immediately began reading a draft resolution against Trotsky to be presented in plenary session. The resolution violently condemned a certain document sent by Trotsky to the political office of the Russian Communist Party. At that meeting of the senior convent the Russian delegation consisted of Stalin, Rikov, Bukharin and Manuilsky, which was extremely unusual. At the end of the reading Thälmann asked us if we agreed with the draft resolution. The Finn Ottomar Kuusinen, the future Quisling of 1941, did not find it strong enough.

"It must be said openly," he suggested, "that the document sent by Trotsky to the political office of the Russian Communist Party has a clearly counterrevolutionary character and is proof that its author has nothing in common with the working class."

Since no one else asked for the floor, after consulting with Togliatti, I apologized to those present for having come late and for not having had a chance to read the document in question.

"Actually," Thälmann candidly remarked, "we haven't seen it either."

Confronted with this all-too-frank reply, I preferred to doubt my ears and repeated my objection in other terms.

"It may very well be," I said, "that the Trotsky document should be condemned, but obviously we can't condemn it until we read it."

"But we haven't read it either," replied Thälmann. "And neither have most of the delegates here, except for the Russians."

Thälmann was speaking German, and his words were being translated into Russian for Stalin and into French for two or three of us. The answer translated to me seemed so incredible that I had words with the translator.

"It's impossible that Thälmann should have said that," I said. "Please give me his answer again, word for word!"

At this point, Stalin intervened. He was standing at one side of the room and seemed to be the only calm and unruffled person in the group.

"The political office of the party has thought it best not to translate Trotsky's document and distribute it to the delegates of the International Executive," Stalin said, "because there are various allusions in it to the policy of the Soviet Government in China."

(Stalin was lying. The mysterious document was published abroad later by Trotsky himself in a pamphlet entitled *Problems of the Chinese Revolution* and, as everyone can now see, it contains no state secrets, but is a violent attack on the China policy of Stalin and the Communist International. In a speech on April 5, 1927, before the Moscow Soviet, Stalin had exalted Chiang Kai-shek and confirmed his faith in the Kuomintang, and that was barely a week before the famous anti-Communist about-face of the Chinese Nationalist head and his party. For this reason the Communists had been suddenly expelled from the Kuomintang, and some tens of thousands of their followers were killed in Shanghai and Wuhan. It is therefore understandable that Stalin did not want a debate about his mistake and tried to protect himself behind "state secrets.")

Ernst Thälmann asked me if Stalin's explanation satisfied me.

"I don't dispute the right of the political office to keep any document secret," I said. "But I don't understand how others can be required to condemn an unknown document."

The indignation against me and Togliatti, who seemed to agree with what I was saying, knew no bounds, especially on the part of the previously mentioned Finn and some Bulgarians and Hungarians.

"This is unheard of," Kuusinen was shouting, red in the face, "that in the citadel of the world revolution we still have such *petit bourgeois!*"

He pronounced the words *"petit bourgeois"* with an extremely comical expression of contempt and disgust. The only person who remained calm and imperturbable was Stalin. He said, "If even one delegate is against the draft resolution, it must not be presented." Then he added, "Perhaps the Italian comrades are not well informed about our internal situation. I suggest we postpone the meeting till tomorrow and that someone here spend the evening with our Italian comrades and explain the situation to them."

The Bulgarian Kolarov was given this unpleasant task. But he took it with courtesy and good nature. He invited us to his

room in the Hotel Lux for a glass of tea that evening, and with
barely any preamble he brought up the thorny problem.

"Let's be frank," he said with a smile. "Maybe you think I've
read the document. No, I haven't read the document. Shall I
tell you the whole truth? The document doesn't even interest
me. Shall I tell you more? Even if Trotsky were to send me a
copy in secret, I would refuse to read it. My dear Italian friends,
this is not a question of documents. I know that Italy is a country of academies, but this is no academy. Here we are, in the
thick of a struggle for power between two rival groups in the
Russian central directorate. Which of these groups do we want
to line up with? That's the question. Documents have nothing
to do with it. It's not a question of finding the historical truth
about the failure of the revolution in China. It's a power struggle between two opposed and irreconcilable groups. We have to
choose. And I've already made up my mind. I'm for the majority group. Whatever the minority does or says, I repeat that I'm
for the majority. Documents don't interest me. We're not in an
academy here."

He refilled our glasses with tea and looked at us like a school-
teacher at two obstreperous boys.

"Have I made myself clear?" he asked, looking straight at
me.

"Yes," I answered, "very clear."

"Have I persuaded you?" he asked me.

"No," I answered.

"Why not?" he wanted to know.

"I'd have to explain why I'm against Fascism," I said.

Kolarov pretended to get indignant, while Togliatti expressed his opinion in more moderate but no less decisive terms.

"You can't come out for the majority or the minority per se,"
he said. "You can't ignore the background of the political
question."

Kolarov listened to him with a benevolent smile of compassion.

"You're still too young," he told us as he accompanied us to

the door. "You don't understand yet what politics is all about."
The following morning, the scene in the senior convent
repeated itself. In the little office where about a dozen of us
were packed like sardines, there was an unusual tension in the
air. Again the Russian delegation was at full strength.

"Have you explained to our Italian comrades what it's all
about?" Stalin asked Kolarov.

"Fully," the Bulgarian assured him.

"If just one delegate is against the draft resolution," Stalin
repeated, "it cannot be presented in the plenary session. A
resolution against Trotsky can be taken only unanimously. Are
our Italian comrades in favor of the draft resolution?" he in-
quired, turning to us.

After consulting with Togliatti, I said, "Before considering
the draft resolution, we will have to be acquainted with the
document it condemns."

The Frenchman Albert Treint and the Swiss Jules Humbert-
Droz made identical statements. (Both of them some years later
also ended up outside the Communist International.)

"The draft resolution is withdrawn," said Stalin.

After that, we went through the same hysterical spectacle of
the day before, with angry and indignant protests from the
various Kuusinens, Rákosis and Peppers.[1] From our scandalous

[1] The substantial truth of this account has been confirmed and justified by
Palmiro Togliatti in the following terms (*Unità*, January 6, 1950):

". . . I come now to the fact which Silone puts at the center of his account
and which he calls scandalous: the meeting of the enlarged Executive of the
Communist International of May, 1927. It generally really went as Silone relates
(except for some minor mistakes which I won't dwell on and which have no
relevance), but I do not understand how he can cite what happened at that
meeting as evidence that the 'Russian power group' was guilty of 'intrigues and
aggression . . . against every independent expression of the other, affiliated
parties.' At the meeting the delegation of the Russian (Bolshevik) party presented a draft resolution against Trotsky and the Trotskyites. The resolution
was such that, had it been approved, it would have meant the exclusion of the
condemned group from the Communist movement. The French, Italian, Swiss
and Spanish delegates (and the Belgians, too, if I remember rightly) stated
that they were still not convinced of the necessity of such a vote. These were
parties which for various reasons were less directly informed of the way in which
the struggle against Trotskyism was being waged in the Russian party. For us
Italian Communists it was a question of whether we were right or wrong, of

attitude Thälmann concluded that our whole anti-Fascist policy in Italy must be wrong, and that if Fascism was still firmly in power it was our fault, and therefore he asked that the policies of the Italian Communist Party be given a rigorous examination.

The inquisitorial examination was postponed until later, and meanwhile the plenary sessions of the Executive began. They were not without their instructive episodes. In the first session an incident occurred which confirmed the seriousness of the differences among the Russian leaders and the brutal indifference with which they were about to be resolved. The meeting had hardly begun when Grigory Zinoviev arrived. Although he was a regular member of the Executive, he was prevented from entering by two uniformed policemen at the door. Leon Trotsky, who was seated next to Togliatti and me, observed the scene, jumped to his feet and denounced the unprecedented outrage.

"Zinoviev is a fully qualified member of this Executive!" he

---

recognizing the necessity of explaining the situation to our members back home and in prison. It was possible to fear, whether rightly or wrongly, I repeat, that a decision taken in the meeting would not be understood by everyone. But what did the Russian comrades do? Silone himself said it: 'If only one delegate,' Stalin said, 'is against the draft resolution, it cannot be presented in the plenary session.' The delegations mentioned did not change their opinion, and the draft was withdrawn. Can you label this conduct 'disloyal,' 'aggressive' or 'suffocating all independent expression'? I don't think so. Since we knew we were all 'in good faith' and since they were also 'in good faith,' the Russian comrades respected our 'freedom' not to be entirely convinced; they allowed us to wait, to 'experiment,' etc., etc.—that is, they did what, according to Silone and other renegades, they were incapable of doing. I have seldom seen such an example of someone who in attacking destroys his attack with his own words and his own example.

"Considering things now, I recognize that our reservations about the Bolsheviks' draft were out of place. Stalin was right; he knew better than we what sort of traitor Trotsky was. And the Executive, which a little later condemned Trotsky severely, had already come to the same conclusion. It had the right to do so, but had we wanted, we could easily have stated our disagreement at no greater risk than that of opening a discussion. Not only did we not do so, since we well understood what turn things were taking, but Silone himself did not even come close to proposing it. As to the merits of the case, history has decided: Stalin's defensive line on the Chinese revolution has brought Mao Tse-tung the victories we all know about. Trotsky became a traitor."

shouted. "Zinoviev, who was elected president of the Comintern on the motion of Lenin and who held the position up to a few months ago, is being kept from this hall by the police!"

For the other members of the Russian delegation the incident obviously was expected and already discounted.

"Zinoviev," said Piatnisky, "resigned as president and as a member of the Executive at the last meeting."

To everyone's surprise Togliatti asked for the floor.

"I was president of that session," he stated. "I was requested by the Russian delegation itself to announce to the assembly that Zinoviev was giving up the position of president, but I was also told to state that he would remain a member of the Executive, since he was named to that job by a congress."

In the meantime Zinoviev had remained on the threshold of the hall, still restrained by the two policemen.

"The incident is closed," Thälmann, who was presiding, said dryly. "It is understood that Zinoviev is no longer a member of the Executive." We were, purely and simply, in a kingdom of arbitrary decisions.

I must confess that my reactions to these incredible episodes were a little rash. They represented not any superior moral virtue, but the naïve spontaneity of the provincial subversive not yet corrupted by cold political calculations. I kept asking Togliatti, "Do you suppose that's the way they do things in the Sacred College of Cardinals? Or in the Fascist Grand Council?" If up to then I had been reserved with Trotsky, who continued to sit next to us in the meetings, I came finally to have precisely the opposite attitude. I had had no special preference for him over Stalin, but that would have been a natural consequence of the outright hate which the cowed creatures of the apparatus showed Trotsky. The latter was no longer what he had appeared the first time I saw him in 1921—the popular head of the Red Army, who had just saved Petrograd—but an old lion trapped in a ditch and on the point of being captured and killed. In the eyes of those who watched him without letup, his every gesture and word took on disproportionate importance.

I remember that during one of the regular sessions I gave Trotsky some copies of a little underground paper from Turin, and he seemed quite touched. He told me of a similar paper, against czarism, which he had edited at Nikolaev when he was still a student. He did not know Italy very well, since he had only passed through, but he remembered it with pleasure, he told me, having enjoyed there a *bella amicizia*. His few words of Italian, in fact, were graceful and had evidently been learned from a woman. Our friendly conversation went on in the pauses in the political debate and during the translations of the speeches. As I have said, it did not go unnoticed by the suspicious members of the apparatus. But my complicity with Trotsky, as well as that of Togliatti, became still more evident when in closing a long and vehement speech in response to some insolence directed at him by the Hungarian Béla Kun, he apologized for concluding with, as he said, some "words in the language of Dante and Togliatti." These words were: "Béla's manners are not very *bella*." Although this joke in Italian was invented by Trotsky (his vocabulary was at least that adequate) and was heard by us with no less surprise than by the others present, it was attributed to us, without anyone bothering to seek confirmation, and added to our other serious political demerits. In fact, it began to get rather "hot" for us, as they say. We were constantly shadowed, and there were other harassments by the police, and annoyed reactions from me. But Togliatti's apparent composure finally calmed me down.

To explain our attitude in that session of the Executive, Togliatti thought it best that the two of us write a letter to the political office of the Russian Communist Party before we left Moscow. No Communist, the letter said in substance, would dare to challenge the pre-eminence of the Russian comrades in the leadership of the International, but this very fact imposed special obligations on the Russians. They should not automatically exert their prerogatives in an authoritarian way. The letter was received by Bukharin, who immediately sent for us, and in a friendly fashion advised us to withdraw it in order not to worsen our already perilous position.

Days of deep discouragement followed for me. Was this the true face of Communism? Were the workers risking their lives and others dying in prison in the service of such an ideal? Was it for this that we led our lonely, dangerous and peripatetic existence as foreigners in our own country?

Behind the façade of the institutions thrown up by the revolution, Russian reality had been profoundly changed, in accordance with a law of decadence of which official doctrine took no account. Was this rapid degeneration into tyranny of one of the greatest revolutions in human history implied in the very principles of Socialism and State ownership? Or was it the result of Leninist ideology and its peculiar organizational form? Or did it simply come from the backward social atmosphere in Russia?

Before I left Moscow, an Italian worker in search of comfort and encouragement came to see me. He had been a refugee in Russia for many years, having fled the sentence of a Fascist tribunal. (I think that he is a Communist to this day.) He came to complain of the humiliating conditions brought about by the workers' ownership of the factory where he was employed. He was willing to put up with material hardships of every kind, since they evidently did not depend on the goodwill of the managers alone. But he said he could not understand why the worker was completely at the mercy of the factory management and had no effective way of defending himself, being in this respect much worse off than workers in capitalistic countries. Most of the much-touted rights of the working class in Russia were purely theoretical. The system's failure was therefore much greater than I had supposed.

During the trip back, in Berlin, I read in the papers that the Comintern Executive had censured Trotsky severely for his report on the events in China. I went to the headquarters of the German Communist Party and asked Thälmann for an explanation. "This is untrue," I said bitterly. "You know they didn't vote for censure." But he explained that in critical cases the statutes of the International authorized the President to adopt any measure in the name of the Executive. They had waited for us to leave Moscow to vote in our name on a text we had not approved. This also explained Stalin's impassivity before the senior convent. (And thus Togliatti's posthumous approval of Stalin's "liberal" conduct assumes a tone of vulgar sarcasm.)

During my few days of enforced idleness in Berlin, while I was waiting for my false documents to be put in order so that I might return to Italy, I read in the papers that the American, Hungarian and Czech Communist parties had vigorously blasted Trotsky's letter.

I asked Thälmann, "So the mysterious document has finally been made public?"

"No," he answered. "But you should learn what Communist discipline means from the American, Hungarian and Czech Communists."

This was said without the remotest suggestion of irony—on the contrary with a lugubrious solemnity entirely appropriate to the nightmare reality to which it referred.

10.

That was in the summer of 1927. I stayed at the center of the party, fully active and holding important positions, until the spring of 1929, when I requested and obtained an indefinite leave of absence for reasons of health. And it was only in the summer of 1931, when I was still politically inactive and after events which I will discuss presently, that I finally broke with the party and was therefore "expelled." How had it been morally possible, after my last visit to Moscow, for me to remain so long in the party? It is a question I have often asked myself. The various reasons were not ignoble. And since I am obligated by my controversy with Togliatti, I want to set them forth, even if discussing them is still painful for me. But in the last analysis, if liberty is dear to me, it is because of what I have suffered to recover it.

When this essay was first published, Togliatti was forced to recite a *mea culpa* in the party newspaper (and I sincerely hope that he won't have to repeat it before a Russian tribunal) for

his grave hesitation, uncertainties and indecisiveness in reject-
ing Bukharinism for Stalinism, that is, a faction in disgrace for a
new and more entrenched majority. I must admit that I was also
going through a crisis at that time, but for a reason which was
precisely the opposite of Togliatti's and with what appears to
have been far greater justification, since it was much harder to
leave the Leninist factions to their fate and return to being
simply a free man. There are disciplined, bureaucratic confes-
sions which are imposed by orthodoxy, and free ones on the part
of those who have conquered their own fear. In determining the
origins and development of questions of conscience the chronology of memory is more dependable than the chronology of
archives. Memory's chronology knows the internal relationships
between facts which appear isolated and remote; it brings them
together and adds stability to the continuity of existence.

The anxiety produced in me by the grotesque episodes in
Moscow in 1927 had less to do with abstract values than with
more urgent and immediate psychological and political considerations. Here, in essence, was one of the many confirmations
of the difficulty of synchronizing European Socialism with Russian Communism, which had fallen into a state of decadence.
And one of the difficulties was surely differences in customs, as
well as differing interpretations of local situations. But only in
its final phase did the conflict present me with an unavoidable
moral choice. It is also interesting to note that of the members
of the Comintern Executive who, in the incident I have just
related, refused to condemn blindly a document they had not
been allowed to read—from the Frenchman Albert Treint to
the Swiss Jules Humbert-Droz—every one but Togliatti later
abandoned the Communist movement, though in different periods from 1928 to 1940, and for complicated personal and
party reasons.

That last trip to Moscow had revealed to me the extreme
complexity and contradictory character of Communism, of
which my personal experience included only one aspect, the

underground struggle against Fascism. My stay in Moscow had shown the other side of the coin. Communism, deriving from the profoundest contradictions in modern society, reproduced them all in itself, with exaggerated virulence, although in a different institutional and social framework. Grouped under its banner were rebels and victims of persecution; heroes and mercenaries; exploiters and exploited; journalists who were risking their lives to bring about unlimited freedom of the press and others who wrote defenses of censorship and the suppression of all opposing publications; accused who invoked elementary judicial guarantees before Fascism's special tribunals and judges who refused the accused any opportunity to prove their innocence; union organizers who fomented strikes in defense of the workers' living standards and others who justified the legal suppression of the right to strike and the adoption of mass forced labor as an integral part of the new economic system; members of Parliament who fought for the widest public control of the government's every action and despots who were practically intractable and immovable, except for those all too frequent instances when they were shot by their own colleagues accused, inevitably, of betrayal.

As may be clear from what I have said, the monstrous ambiguity of Communism resulted from the different positions of power occupied by the various groups, but this fact did not justify the conclusion that it was all one way in Russia and entirely opposite elsewhere. But certainly on my way back from Russia, I passed through areas where the Communists were simple left-wing Socialists, until finally in the workers and farmers of France, Switzerland and Italy I found those traits of generosity, frankness, solidarity and lack of prejudice which were the genuine and traditional resource of Socialism in its struggle against bourgeois decadence and corruption. The remembered events of Moscow seemed like an unreal nightmare when I was back in the company of those Communists.

When I discussed this in a small underground meeting in Milan, the first reaction was incredulity, followed by the naïve proposal to print posters reading "Long Live Trotsky" and paste them on the walls of Milanese factories. But more sensible ideas finally prevailed, and it was one of those who was to join the Trotskyite group two years later who made the most trenchant suggestion. "The sphere of our responsibility," Pietro Tresso, one of our best underground leaders, wrote in a letter to me, "is Italy, not Russia. We cannot jeopardize our struggle against Fascism just because the Russians are fighting among themselves. At first glance the conditions of the struggle in Italy and in Russia seem to suggest they represent the beginning and end, respectively, of the same journey. But it would be impossible to establish a faithful connection between these two points. Therefore let us go forward and let us hope that the future Communist revolution in Italy will end up a little better." I answered that I agreed completely with the spirit of his comment. "I have no reverence for historical inevitability," I wrote him. "And in this situation Lenin's maxim is relevant: the true revolutionary is recognized by the way he acts in his own country."

I had to come to an agreement with Togliatti in exactly these terms before we separated. Hanging over us, was the Damocles' sword of an investigation by the Executive of our political orientation and administration, in reprisal for Togliatti's Bukharinist sympathies and for our scandalous attitude at the Moscow meetings. But how, when and to whom the job would be entrusted was impossible to predict, since the factional struggle was still raging in Moscow. It was not our mission, nor was it in our power, to influence the Muscovite conflict. But it was our duty and within our power, if we stayed together, to defend our organization and policies from invalid criticisms and firmly to oppose unjustified changes and deviations. Togliatti seemed sincerely committed to this, even though in private meetings he insisted a little too much on the unanimity clause, justifying himself with the recent example of the Spanish Communist Party. Although the majority of its members opposed Moscow's arbitrary demands, the party had been dissolved and some young men of the minority had been appointed to re-establish it. Such a minority capable of accepting a nod from Moscow to bring its own party to heel existed in Italian Communism as well, and was represented even then by Longo and Secchia. In other words, Togliatti put solidarity with these comrades above the possible defense of our rights against Moscow's tyranny. It is important to recall that, in spite of marked local differences, Communist parties in other countries were beset by the same difficulties.

11.

The position we adopted under the circumstances, though dictated by necessity, was patently ambiguous, timid and in the long run untenable. The only ones who did not suffer from these complications were the "home based" Communists engaged in Italian underground activities, who refused to trust the newspaper accounts of the differences among the Russian leaders—to the point that one of their papers branded as a lie the news, reported by the Fascist press, that Trotsky had been deported to Alma-Ata in Central Asia. But the predicament of the leaders of the party abroad, and especially those with international jobs, was not easy. Togliatti was shrewd enough, in front of other party leaders, to refuse a post in the leadership of a planned European branch of the Comintern with headquarters in Berlin, even though Manuilsky came personally to invite him. And he was clever enough to induce Angelo Tasca, a man he detested and of whom he was jealous, to accept the job of new permanent delegate to Moscow, thus exposing him to certain danger. We had entered into a period of crude and primitive relationships, in which cunning was more useful than intelligence and problems in tactics were substituted for questions of principle. At a certain point it became clear that the punitive mission of the Executive of the Comintern against us (motivated by the well-known political ties between Togliatti and Bukharin) had been postponed to allow the elimination of leftist opposition in Russia, before attacking more moderate elements. This, of course, was in accordance with the ancient tactic of defeating one's adversaries one at a time, and for us it meant an unexpected moratorium of two years.

The final scenes of the tragedy are well known. After another year of polemics and violent clashes, Stalin ascended the remaining steps to absolute power by deporting Trotsky to Alma-Ata and dismissing from their jobs, or transferring far from Moscow, other leaders of the leftist bloc gathered around Trotsky, Zinoviev and Kamenev. And to keep the summit of the pyramid under the uncontested control of Stalin and his group, the battle was immediately joined to subdue or destroy the remaining currents of the right, first of all those of Bukharin. Fighting them where they were strongest—among the farmers— Stalin thus announced the forced collectivization of small and medium-sized agricultural properties which had been set up with difficulty after 1923, in line with Lenin's new economic policy. Six or seven million peasants were driven from their farms, killed or deported to Siberia and forced labor.

Of the truly Babylonian aspects of this war against the peasants we knew little. Nor was precise information on the cruelty with which it was waged available to us while it was in course, although later many of the facts were made public. But even the little we knew at the time would have been enough to arouse resentment and opposition among many of us, had not our judgment and will been victimized by our a priori policy of not provoking a crisis in the underground organization over a problem foreign to the immediate experience of the members. And so, to begin with, when Angelo Tasca returned from Moscow to tell us how as our representative he had been led to assume a position openly critical of Stalin's agricultural policy, we were very ill at ease, and as Italian Communists we refused to enter a conflict with the Russian Communist Party and the International. To have done so would have been to risk divisions in our ranks on a question which by its very nature could not be presented to our party cells for judgment. Behind the screen, by no means fictitious, of our national responsibility, which was a thousand times more important to us, we evaded a difficult but inescapable international duty, victims in our turn of the gross sophistry of the Bulgarian Vasil Kolarov, whom we had ridiculed two years before. Thus even those of us who agreed with Angelo Tasca and were his friends made the cowardly mistake of isolating and condemning him. Our conduct might have been justified if, the year after, when the Moscow Executive attacked and condemned all our policies from 1924 on (namely, all the policies inspired by Antonio Gramsci), we had stuck together solidly in defending them, as we had originally planned. But the demoralization suffered during that long period of ambiguity and equivocation, the mistrust toward those among us who seemed most likely to surrender to Moscow's every claim, as well as the example of what was happening in other parties, finally produced the opposite effect. And even those few who, taken unawares, protested and were expelled from the party found themselves acting under extremely confused and painful conditions, with no possibility of expressing themselves on the real background of the problem. What was more serious, they did not realize the real meaning of their acts and their consequences. How could we have deluded ourselves into thinking that a serious examination of the controversial issues could be carried out in good faith in a totalitarian system? Our surprise showed how ignorant we were of the real nature of developments in Russian and in international Communism during recent years and how imperfect was our perception of the tangle of contradictions in which we found ourselves involved.

The truth is that you don't free yourself from the Communist Party the way you resign from the Liberal Party, chiefly because your ties with the party are in proportion to the sacrifices they exact. And further, as we have noted, for its active members the Communist Party is not merely, or even mainly, a political organization, but school, church, barracks and family. It is a totalitarian institution in the fullest sense of the word and requires the total allegiance of those who submit to it. Every totalitarian organism, every regime of coerced humanity, involves a large dose of lies, duplicity and insincerity. The sincere Communist, on the other hand, who by some miracle retains his inborn critical faculty and persists in applying it to the party's doings, in the belief that in this way he is of greater use to it, exposes himself to the painful hardships of nonconformity and, before he is able to take a final step in the direction either of total submission to the party or total freedom in renunciation of the party, he must suffer the torments of hell in his innermost being. The very slowness with which he becomes aware of his heresy's implications is revealing. As long as he operates in the same psychological sphere as the authority with which he is in conflict, he can maintain the illusion that his dissent is limited to this or that single issue on which he wants to argue in the name of common principles, insisting on the purity of their origin. But if later, freed of every disciplinary bond by excommunication or expulsion, and ostracized from the community of the faithful, he finds the courage to argue from effects to causes, and if he wishes to understand what in the final analysis prevented his total capitulation, he will realize that his disobedience actually obeyed more obscure dictates, and the dogmas he used to venerate will suddenly appear to him in a new light. To conclude: one is cured of Communism the way one is cured of a neurosis.

12.

The repression of the moderate currents in Russian Communism was extended simultaneously to all sections of the International in a complete swerve to the left of its entire policy, motivated by an alleged world revolutionary crisis then in progress. The new tactic, according to its supporters, was directed chiefly at freeing the spirit of the workers from the debilitating illusions of democracy. Parliamentary democracy was therefore denounced as the biggest obstacle in the path of the proletarian revolution, and its disappearance was seen as a sign of progress. Traditional Democratic Socialism was rebaptized Social Fascism, in other words a simple faction or variety of Fascism, and every accommodation with it was to be severely condemned. Consequently, even union solidarity with the reformists was to be broken in the few countries where it survived, and in its place Red unions under Communist direction were to be set up. The result of that insane new tactic (a result which symbolizes all the others) occurred some years later, and was of decisive help in bringing Hitler to power. In line with the new tactics, an official publication of the Communist International, *International Correspondence*, called the advent of Nazism a step forward for the proletarian revolution since it eliminated every democratic illusion from the German political horizon. Translated into the language of Italian politics, this new policy arrogantly ordered from Moscow amounted to a radical negation of the entire Communist policy of the previous few years. And it was explicitly commanded by emissaries from the International sent for the purpose of confirming it. Most of the Italian Communist leaders submitted to this tyranny and accepted the condemnation of Gramsci's theses on the Italian situation. At this point one might well ask whether any collective resistance to these unjustified demands on Italian Communism would have been possible. But this is a completely abstract question. The very lack of unanimity among the leaders which was cited by those in power as the *sine qua non* for such an attempt relieved the leaders from the responsibility of resistance.

For reasons of health I had been absent from party work for more than a year. I had been kept informed on the progress of the internal crisis by private letters and visits. But even those who took part in all the meetings were no less surprised than I at the final solution. Three of the best men in our organization —Alfonso Leonetti, leader of the underground press; Paolo Ravazzoli, leader of the union movement; and Pietro Tresso, head of the administrative office—criticized the International's demands, pointing out their absurdity with respect to the situation in Italy. For their audacity, they were summarily expelled from the Central Committee, and later from the ranks of the party. For grotesque reasons utterly without foundation, they were offered as scapegoats to Moscow's spite toward Togliatti's Bukharinist past. Unfortunately, the three who were expelled soon expressed themselves in acts and words which seemed to justify the measures which had been taken against them. No doubt they were driven by burning resentment for their unjust and unexpected treatment, and by the very logic of such factional controversy.

One day in a village not far from the Swiss town where I was living I had a visit from Togliatti. At great length he explained, clearly and loyally, the reasons for the line of conduct he had chosen after mature reflection. The present state of the International, he said in substance, was certainly neither pleasant nor satisfactory. It didn't depend on our goodwill to change it. It was a question of objective historical conditions, to which we had to submit. The forms of the proletarian revolution were not arbitrary. If they did not correspond to our prejudices, all the worse for us. And on the other hand what was the alternative? What had been the fate up to then of Communists who broke with their party? To what disastrous circumstances had Social Democracy been reduced? My objections to these arguments I must say, were not very pertinent, especially since Togliatti's reasoning was exclusively political, but the disturbances produced within me by my recent experiences went beyond politics. What were the "inexorable historical forms" to which we had to bow, if not a new image of the inhuman behavior against which we had rebelled when we had called ourselves Socialists? For the sake of the struggle, could we forget the reasons for which we had entered it in the first place? To do so was to act like someone who has had a terrific blow on the head and continues to stand, walk, talk and gesture without fully knowing what is going on.

I announced to Togliatti my intention of staying in the party, excused from all political activity. As soon as my health allowed it, I would accept some secondary position as an assistant or editor, but not anything more. Togliatti said he agreed with that. The reasons for my perplexity were very complicated, personal as well as political. In the émigré press the controversy over the party and the three who had been expelled had taken on a disgusting bitterness and vulgarity. Men who had been friends up to a short time before, united against a common danger, were calling each other traitors, cowards, liars, opportunists, hypocrites and even thieves, spies and mercenaries. I was horrified at the very idea of doing something, however necessary and inevitable, which might cause people I liked to attack me with lies and insults and require me to respond in kind. If only it were possible to disappear in silence.

There was an even more serious reason, which it is not easy for me to discuss. My younger brother, the last one I had left, had been in jail in Italy for more than two years, since April, 1928, accused of being a member of the illegal Communist Party. At the time of his arrest he had been brutally tortured, receiving permanent internal injuries. It was not until 1932, in the penitentiary at Procida, that death put an end to his pain. But the thing which made his fate especially poignant was that, at least up to the moment of his arrest, he had never been a member of the Communist Party, had never asked to be a member, had never been admitted, had never taken part in any of its meetings or activities, and did not even know its rules or program. He was a vaguely anti-Fascist young man whose education and feelings were Catholic. He was far more interested in sport than in politics, and sport had added to his natural pride a particularly keen sense of honor. Why did he confess that he was a Communist? Why did he affirm his confession before the judge of a special tribunal which used his confession to condemn him to twelve years in prison? He wrote me: "I have tried to act as I thought you would have in my place." So it was not easy for me to leave the party, if my presence in it might serve to justify my brother's sacrifice.

But passive membership, without making retractions and

condemning expelled "traitors," was not a course approved by
the Comintern. In a meeting at Moscow whose minutes Togliatti sent me, a Russian delegate in fact charged the Italian party
with such behavior. Togliatti came to visit me in Switzerland
again, accompanied by another man. This time our meeting
took place at the headquarters of the "Soccorso Rosso" in Zü-
rich. I am obliged to report it in some detail since the Communist press has given a distorted version of the encounter.

"It is essential that you issue a statement condemning the
three who have been expelled," Togliatti said to me, "and submitting absolutely to the discipline of the International."

"You know perfectly well that that is against my convictions," I answered.

"I know," he told me. "But accepting this kind of coercion is
a worthy sacrifice to the party."

To spare me the physical act at least, he sat down at a type-
writer and wrote five or six lines of prescribed statements and
himself typed my party name below. It probably seemed to both
Togliatti and me that by this ceremony I was drinking deep of
the disgusting purge; but that is not the way it was.

I was still carrying on a friendly correspondence with Pietro
Tresso, one of those who had been expelled. I did not conceal
from him my apprehensions about the choice he had made together with the others: adherence to the international Trotskyite faction. And with all sincerity I listed my personal reasons
for preferring to remain at the edge of the party, saying nothing, approving neither Trotsky's policies nor the new orders
from Moscow. These personal letters were passed on by Tresso
to some of his Trotskyite friends, to keep them informed. But
without the knowledge of either of us, they published excerpts
in the Trotskyite bulletin in Paris, omitting everything personal and suppressing everything against Trotskyism. This had
wider repercussions than had been counted on. In the eyes of
the party these letters "proved" that I was playing a double
game and showed that I secretly belonged to the Trotskyites and
thus had not been sincere in issuing the statement Togliatti

had extracted from me. I was immediately warned that a new delegation, this time headed by Ruggero Grieco, was coming to Switzerland to question me. I was told: "You will be asked for a new and more binding statement. You will be asked to take an active part in the campaign against the Trotskyites. You will be asked to return to the headquarters of the party and take on a responsible job." We had come to the summer of 1931. I had been away from party activity for more than two years.

I could have defended myself. I could have established my good faith. I could have proved that I did not belong to the Trotskyite faction. I could have shown that my disagreement with the new orders from Moscow was shared by the very men who had been assigned to question me. I could have told them what had happened when Togliatti requested the statement and I had "issued" it. I could have persuaded them that I was completely indifferent to posts and hierarchies. I could have, but I did not want to. In one flash, I had the clearest realization that all cleverness, cunning and compromise would simply be futile. A month later, two years later, I would be right back where I started. It was better to finish it off once and for all. I must not let slip this providential opportunity, this "emergency exit." There was no sense staying there arguing. It was over. Thank God.

13.

As is known, Communist parties do not tolerate resignations. They recognize only expulsions. Like the sentences of Russian tribunals in political trials, announcements of expulsion from the Communist Party have a high polemic value. The terms "treason," "betrayal" and "bribery" are simply synonyms for opposition. The defamation varies according to the victim's importance.

The formula adopted in my case might seem to be one of the most benign, compared with the inevitable defamation practiced in Russia and elsewhere in order to liquidate hundreds of thousands of schismatic or heretical Communists by expulsion, deportation or execution. Party practice allows for no political dissidence whatsoever. In a certain sense I suggested the formula for myself. Among those in the delegation which came to visit me was Giuseppe di Vittorio. In a benevolent and almost friendly way, he enumerated the difficulties of every variety I would run into outside the party.

"You can't go back to Italy as long as Fascism is in power," he told me. "You can't stay abroad without papers. You have no means of making a living. Your health is not good. Your brother is in jail on account of the party. All your friends are in the party and would break with you as soon as you left it. There is no opposition but ours to Fascism. So if you have the least common sense, if you can still think and act like a normal person . . ."

At this point, I interrupted him. "Listen," I said. "I don't know if you can understand, but in the sense in which you're using the word I've never been and probably never will be a politically normal person."

I left the meeting, saying we really had nothing more to say to each other. In the expulsion notice that followed, after a thoroughly sanitized account of the episodes I have just related, came the words: " . . . since he himself has admitted that he is politically abnormal, a clinical case . . . etc."

It was an abusive and defamatory document. Its very authors did not believe it, of course; otherwise they would not have made that last attempt to keep me in the party. It was a polemical weapon intended to neutralize anything I might do in the future threatening the unity of the party. When, in fact, I did not, and the possibility of my return to, or at least my collaboration with, the party was being considered, the very men who had issued the defamatory expulsion notice authorized another, benevolent, unofficial and oral version of my separation. It was said to have been the regrettable consequence of a moment of discouragement and pessimism over the anti-Fascist struggle.

One or the other of the two versions (the official one referring to the political renegade and the unofficial one referring to the pessimist) was subsequently used depending on whether my writings and speeches pleased or irritated the Communists. Neither of the two is correct. Neither is of the least use in revealing the heart of the crisis which took me out of the party. I myself became aware of it only gradually and painfully over the course of the succeeding years. And I continue to ponder it even today, in an attempt to understand it better. If I have written books as I have already said, it was to try to understand and to make others understand. I am not at all sure that I have come to the end of my reflections.

The truth is this: my exit from the Communist Party was a very sad day for me, a day of mourning, of mourning for my youth. And where I come from, mourning is worn longer than elsewhere. It is not easy to free oneself from so intense an experience as Communism. Something of it always remains to mark one's character for the rest of one's life. Look how recognizable ex-Communists are. They form a unique category, like ex-priests and former career officers. The number of ex-Communists is legion. "The final struggle," I said to Togliatti one day, "will be between the Communists and the ex-Communists."

This statement was widely discussed later. But the meaning I attribute to it is simple. What I meant was that perhaps the experience of Communism itself would kill Communism. And it is possible that the Russians themselves are in the process of administering the *coup de grâce*. What will happen when the millions who have returned from the forced labor camps of Siberia are able to speak freely?

After leaving the party, I carefully avoided landing in one of the numerous groups of ex-Communists, and that I do not regret. I know the fatalism which dominates them and makes them into little sects with all the defects of official Communism—fanaticism, centralism and abstraction—without the characteristics and advantages which in Communism derive from the presence of large numbers of workers. The logic of opposition at all costs has led many ex-Communists far from where they started out, even to Fascism. But a dispassionate critique of my experience has led me to a better understanding of the reasons for my separation and to the conclusion that they go well beyond the immediate causes.

What have I left from this long and sad adventure? A secret affection for some men I knew in the party and the ashen taste of a wasted youth. The initial mistake—of hoping to obtain from political action something it cannot give—was certainly mine. Even a revolt inspired by the desire for freedom can be a trap, yet it is better than supine acceptance of one's fate. Whenever I reflect calmly on these misfortunes, I feel rise within me an unhappy bitterness which might have been impossible for me to escape.

14.

My faith in Socialism (I suppose my subsequent conduct bears witness to it) has remained more alive than ever. In its essentials it has returned to what it was when I first rebelled against the old social order: an extension of the ethical requirements of the restricted individual and family sphere to the entire realm of human activity; a need for effective brotherhood; an affirmation of the priority of the human person above all the economic and social mechanisms which oppress him. With the passage of years there has been added a reverence for that which incessantly drives mankind to surpass itself and which is at the root of his unallayable anxiety. But I do not mean to press for my own brand of Socialism. The "insane truths" I mentioned are far older than Marxism. Around the second half of the last century they found a home in the workers' movement which had been spawned by industrial capitalism, and they continue to remain one of its most enduring sources of inspiration. Every sincere Socialist, whether he is aware of it or not, believes in them. I have often expressed my view of the relationships between the Socialist movement and theories of Socialism. They are not all rigid or immutable. They are the same relationships that are to be found between philosophical schools and the great movements of history. As they are studied and analyzed, the theories can die out and be repudiated, but the movement goes on. I am convinced that Socialism will outlive Marxism. It would be inaccurate, however, to number me among the empiricists in the traditional quarrel between doctrinaires and empiricists in the workers' movement. I cannot conceive of Socialism tied to any particular theory, only to a faith. The more Socialist theories claim to be "scientific," the more transitory they are. But Socialist values are permanent. The distinction between theories and values is still not clearly enough understood by those who ponder these problems, but it is fundamental. A school or a system of propaganda may be founded on a collection of theories. But only on a system of values can one construct a culture, a civilization, a new way of living together as men.

September–October, 1949

VI

The Situation of the "Ex"

In the multitude of refugees who have come to Switzerland from just about everywhere in Europe, there are some of a special kind, who, although scattered in various places of internment, constitute a category by themselves. They have in common—or, to be more precise, we have in common—not a country of origin, or a language, or a religion, nor even an identical political position, but an experience. We are considered, and we really are, Exes. The experience referred to by the word "Ex" has certainly not annihilated our individuality, but it has marked us, at least for a time, in a way that we have no reason to hide.

Some aspects of our situation are, to say the least, bizarre. In a period in which a man is defined largely by his passport, we have none. For obvious reasons we are denied them by the consulates of our countries of origin, as well as by our former party, which, because of the needs of its underground, is notorious for giving serious competition to our consulates. Not only would it be foolish for us to expect help from either of these offices; we must be on our guard because both of them pursue us relentlessly. As you know, the Swiss police keep us registered on a separate list appropriately called the list of the "Schriftenlosen" ("Paperless"), a status which involves numerous obligations in return for the right of asylum. With great prudence, the authorities have entrusted the surveillance of the "Paperless" to functionaries carefully chosen from among the least imaginative, which causes us endless additional complications and annoyances. But, luckily for us, Switzerland's official neutrality does not imply the neutrality of the minds and hearts of its citizens.

In our temporary situation we have every kind of major and minor difficulty to contend with, even of the most primitive kind, about which ordinary mortals know nothing. Our names, to begin with—what do we call ourselves? Many of us have had to decide that question on our own. In spite of the stupidity of our enemies, we have never been able to use the name of No Man as Ulysses did with Polyphemus. We have always had a first and last name. But the trouble is that we have acquired too many names as the need for them arose, and one of them, probably not the most pleasant, has stuck. And so it sometimes happens that we do not recognize in a certain person a common friend, simply because each of us has known him under a different name. The rule of the underground requires the activist, as a protective measure, to give up the name listed with the Bureau of Vital Statistics so as to sidetrack or slow up police investigation. But the effect on personal identity can be even more far-reaching. As in the case of the monk when he enters an order, the adoption of a party name when one passes outside the law signifies for the "professional revolutionary" a break with his family and every private relationship, and his installation in a separate world. Leaving it is like a small death. This is why the traumatic situation of the ex-Communist recalls that of the ex-monk.

After years of using false papers and borrowed names, it is odd suddenly to reacquire one's original name. This name can easily seem stranger and more unreal than the others we have used, since it brings back the years in which we were not entirely ourselves. I suppose that many take back their legal names like an nth pseudonym, for some new and urgent purpose.

Each of us came to break with the party, I think we can confess without false shame, in his own way—and nearly all of us in the worst way, that is, without the fine rationalization we would be able to write now. No; the act of liberation we now boast about was achieved, by some more so and by others less, unwillingly and confusedly, and on accidental, sometimes trifling grounds: questions of tactics, of priorities, perhaps the delusion that we were the true Communists. Only later, looking back, did we become convinced of the absolute necessity of the break and of the internal maturing which made it impossible to delay any longer. Now, probably, we ask ourselves how we could have possibly stayed so long *"en cette galère."* Who would be likely to concede our good faith? Perhaps only an ex-monk.

As Exes we have a painful duty to perform. It is not pleasant to talk about oneself, about one's own mistakes, stupidities and moments of hysteria. It is no fun to relive those nightmare years, even in memory. But we must bear witness. Many have entered the party because of us. Our first duty is to them; our next is to the young who are looking for a banner or a cause. What are we to say? Simply the truth. The truth is not a series of scandalous revelations for which the giant news services are so hungry, but the tragic reality which lies behind the façade of Communism and which is an essential element of our era.

If I think back now to the young Italian and other comrades I met right after the First World War in international meetings of Communist youth, and to the fellowship which then bound us together, the courageous solidarity which ignored international boundaries, and the burning hope for a new, freer and more humane order, it is not the bitter defeat that met us in Italy and Germany that disturbs me most, it is not the memory of Gastone Sozzi killed in the prisons of Perugia, of Eugen Schönhaar decapitated in Berlin, of Gramsci dying in the internment camp at Turi, nor of other worthy and honest militants for the common ideal; it is something completely different and far more obscure and complicated. Against the background of the monstrous Moscow trials, in which all the surviving leaders of the October Revolution presented themselves as spies, traitors and imperialist agents, there was the deportation of millions of workers to the concen-

tration camps of Siberia; the assassination of Vuyovic, founder
of Communist Youth in Yugoslavia; the suicide in Moscow of
Schatzky, head of the Russian Communist Youth; the assassination in Spain of Andrès Nin and Camillo Berneri; the still
mysterious hanging of Willi Münzenberg in a wood near Mar-
seille; the depression and hopeless disgust in which some of the
survivors of that elect group vegetate here and there throughout
the world.

It would have been too easy to do as some advised us and
pontificate in the face of so much tragedy, "History will judge!"
and then remain silent. Yes, we know some who are waiting for
this Nemesis the way one waits for a bus. There is no doubt that
those who follow us will pass judgment. And if the reporters are
only allowed to record the bare facts and the explanations of the
victims' friends and those of the executioners' assistants, some
small relief may be found in the hope that it may one day be
possible to know the whole truth and that just men will render
dispassionate judgment. But we were directly involved. We
were neither reporters nor historians and we could not remain
silent. We were not attracted by "posterity." Being justly jealous of the use made of our lives, we could not cease living while
awaiting the judgment of posterity. When our friends and comrades began killing themselves, we could not parrot the pre-
fabricated explanations of the propaganda releases, nor could
we wash our hands of the matter. In the disorder in which we
were involved, we wanted to see each other clearly. To continue
living, hoping and struggling, we absolutely had to know the
value of the cause to which we had consecrated our lives. (We
had only one life to give and we could not give it up lightly.)
We needed to know what the new political and economic order
they proposed in place of the old bourgeois order was really
worth to mankind. And how could we plausibly explain that in
our ranks were to be found both martyrs and mercenaries,
fighters for liberty as well as inquisitors, rebels and police spies?
How was it possible for those who so eloquently defended the
sacred rights of the individual against the Fascist dictatorship to

judge those same rights as *petit bourgeois* prejudices when they
or their comrades were in power? It was clear that in ourselves,
in our movement, in our doctrine, side by side with love and
respect for man resided hate and contempt, and that a vocation
for tyranny nestled next to the desire for liberty. In spite of a
thousand emotional ties which kept us in the movement and
which we would have liked to preserve, this duplicity was insupportable to us. We could no longer hesitate in the choice
between the GPU and its victims.

Then, too, at one point, we were no longer sustained by the
argument that every new order demands sacrifices. What new
order? For those of us who had the opportunity to see it close
up, the Russian dictatorship appeared in its naked reality: a
system of oppression and exploitation of a new kind. The seeds
of Socialism which bloomed in the October Revolution had
been smothered by a bureaucratic totalitarian state. There was
no further trace of the Soviets or other forms of popular control. The social inequalities were as scandalous as elsewhere.
Consumption of the fruits of labor for the state and for arma-
ments was extremely high. What was most revolting was the fact
that the workers had no defense because the very unions were
on the State's side. We heard of spontaneous strikes during
which the workers were attacked as much by the trade-union
bureaucracy as by the police.

Someone will protest, "Is it possible to carry on such criticism in time of war? Wouldn't it be prudent to postpone it?" If
we only knew who is going to win this damned war. We don't
even know whether the much-feared Nazi invasion of Switzerland will take place. If it does, we will run the risk of being
captured by the Germans and deported. And so forth. These are
serious questions, to which everyone will give the answers he
thinks correct. In our circumstances, no one of us can give
orders to anyone else, and no one would be obliged to obey
them; but we can consult with one another. After mature reflection I have reached the conclusion that prudence at best may
condition our acts, but not our consciences. As for me, I will say

more. We are a group of friends, Italians, who, although looking with sympathy on the Allied cause, do not intend to identify
ourselves with it. We are carrying on a private war against
Fascism, which preceded the war among nations and will continue after it, whatever the outcome of that war. The fight
against the danger of totalitarianism will certainly not end with
this war.[1] It is in this perspective that our present difficulties
must be seen. To face them decently, if you will excuse the
expression, it is necessary, before anything else, to be at peace
with one's conscience. After that, if one is involved in a
struggle, there is just one tried and true remedy against panic,
and that is to fight. But, in speaking to Exes, I want to add: the
past, with the deep wounds it has left us, must not be an excuse
for weakness. We must not allow ourselves to be demoralized by
blows, by laziness or by written or spoken stupidities. From the
moment our will is pure, a new strength can be drawn from the
worst in us. *"Etiam peccata."*

This way of thinking may seem religious to some, and not
wrongly so. The word does not make me blush since it does not
express a sentiment but an awareness. I have already said on
other occasions that I consider the rediscovery of the Christian
heritage in the ferment of liberation taking place in contemporary society our most important spiritual gain. I think this is
very apparent in *Bread and Wine* and *The Seed Beneath the
Snow*.[2] In reviewing these two novels, an American critic attempted to establish a direct relationship between Pietro Spina
and that group of Russian Socialists who emerged after the
defeat of the Revolution of 1905, who were called the "God-
seekers." I hope it will not seem presumptuous if I attempt to

[1] Silone refers here to a document called "Theses of the Third Front," which
he edited for the Foreign Center of the Italian Socialists and which appeared in
the August 1, 1941, edition of the Italian-language periodical *L'Avvenire dei
lavoratori*, published in Zurich. (See Aldo Garosci, *Storia dei fuorusciti*, ed.
Laterza Bari, 1953, pp. 283–284, and the chapter "Nel bagaglio dell'esule" in
Esperienze e studi socialisti, Scritti in onore di Ugo G. Mondolfo, La Nuova
Italia Editrice, Florence, 1957, pp. 301–315.)

[2] New York, Atheneum, 1962 and 1965, respectively, translated by Harvey
Fergusson II.

explain that there is little in common between the two positions. As in the poem of Francis Thompson, I have the impression that Pietro Spina is not seeking God, but that he is being
pursued by Him, as one can be by one's shadow or something
within oneself:

> I hid from Him, and under running laughter.
> Up vistaed hopes I sped;
> And shot, precipitated,
> Adown Titanic glooms of chasmèd fears,
> From those strong Feet that followed, followed after.

In the Gospel, furthermore, it is God Who seeks man: *"Quaerens
me sedisti lassus."* I would like to add my feeling that in Pietro
Spina's conscience "the tranquil step with weighted insistence"
resounds in moments of strength, not of weakness. The difference seems to me worth noting. To avoid misunderstanding, let
me insist on this difference.

The so-called religious revival is characterized by the usual
fact that it follows disaster and defeat. Every historical defeat
brings with it humiliation for man, creating in him anew a lack
of self-confidence, confronting him once more with his weakness, incapacity, misery and guilt. And there are those who use
the defeat as proof that human history obeys inflexible laws, in
which there is no place for rebellion or aggression. In every
religious revival which follows a period of defeats and humilia-
tions there is, on one hand, the poignant nostalgia of the
prodigal son, reduced to looking after the pigs in his father's
dilapidated house, and, on the other, the Machiavellian ruling
classes who are themselves unbelieving and cynical at heart, yet
know from long experience that the best policeman to keep
men in a state of submission is the fear of God. But Pietro Spina
considers those men atheists, not believers, who say, "We need
God," in the same way one says, "We need armored cars and
more meat." And I do not think that Pietro Spina has the
slightest nostalgia for his father's house. However the present
war comes out, it is not likely that he will end up submitting.

Those of you who are writers know by experience how certain characters can become aggressive and wind up dominating the author. Now, writing and thinking of Pietro Spina, I have the impression that his feeling for God leads him not to resignation, but to courage and even rashness.

It remains for me now to give you my frank opinion of the two curses which the party hurls at us at the moment of our departure. "You are condemned to the most squalid isolation," it shouts to us, "to a complete break with any form of socialism and democracy." Well, these gloomy predictions do indeed have an intimidating effect on certain weak spirits, just as in countries governed by the Communists the lot of the Ex is even worse than that of the excommunicated in the Middle Ages. But in the rest of the world we should answer with confidence that our fate depends on ourselves alone. Without making any concessions to the spirit of the argument, I can guarantee that, as far as I am concerned, I rediscovered a genuine rapport with others only after I had left the party. Why should the normal man need an intermediate apparatus to communicate with his fellow man? Anyone who thinks he escapes solitude by participating in totalitarian meetings grossly deceives himself. There is really no more grotesque sight than that of worn-out, decadent artists trying to find a fictitious youth by getting in step with the Fascists or Communists.

In every period and under every regime men's true isolation is produced by lies, envy and egotism. There is a serious threat of isolation, a threat I would call an occupational hazard, which strikes writers and artists in particular, and it is a direct consequence of narcissism. But no party card can grant immunity from this pernicious malady of the spirit. Actually, a personal disposition to be sociable, sympathetic and generous, which can go as far as a feeling that others are really present in us, is a fact of human consciousness to which party bureaucracies can add nothing of importance.

But it is inevitable that there will be no common view on further participation in political life among the Exes. Any reflections on that point will therefore be even more personal. While some of my friends have become Trotskyites, and others Social Democrats, I, as you know, have been unable to see my way clear to moving directly from one political militancy to another, although I have in my own way remained a free-lance Socialist. (I consider anti-Fascism to be a simple corollary of this.) But the term "Socialism" is now so wide and indefinite that it means nothing precise any more. It is no exaggeration to say that it all must be thought through again, and the pseudo-scientific nineteenth-century baggage which Socialism is barely able to drag along with it should be put aside.

The fate of Socialism after the First World War was like that of the hunter who went hunting for quail and ran into wolves. The Socialists were convinced that there were no more wolves, at least in civilized countries. Marxism, in fact, made no allowance for them. Even less foreseeable was the fact that when faced with certain difficulties of climate and food, many Socialists themselves yielded to the call of the wild and became ferocious in turn. In the struggle with the wolves, to save ourselves some of us were obliged to go beyond our nineteenth-century, bourgeois limitations and rediscover our paleo-Christian heritage. In essence this consists of the permanent validity of certain moral values designed to rescue mankind's communal living from the laws of the jungle. I have written on another occasion that our soul has depths excavated by pain, which we were unaware of in 1919.

One of the tragedies of our time has been the degeneration of Marxism in those countries where its partisans have gained the upper hand: from the ruthless condemnation of ideology it has passed to the most dogmatic of ideologies; from a proclamation of the priority of man over things it has changed into a cold technocracy; and from a movement of political liberation it has turned into a system of slavery. When we were still in the party, if we tried to argue with Russian Marxists, we had the impression of talking with somnambulists. They used Marxism as a drug to dull sensibility and to make pain more bearable. The future revolution in Russia will probably have among its slogans: Marxism is the opiate of the people. (There is no doubt that the seeds of a new revolution have been sown in Russia even if no one can tell whether it will break out in ten years or in a century.) More important is the fact that no theory is exclusively revolutionary or progressive, and that every revolutionary theory is susceptible to reversal in the direction of reaction. All that need happen is for it to fall into the hands of a power group, and they will use it as an instrument for their domination.

The fate of Socialism or Communism, I hasten to add, is in my opinion by no means tied to Marxism. Socialism or Communism is a permanent aspiration of the human spirit, which thirsts after social justice. In its essence it is an extension of the moral criteria of private life to all social life. It is an ideal for the further humanization of our earthly existence by bringing under man's domination the economic forces which tend to oppress him. This ideal, like all great human aspirations, has assumed various forms and justifications in the course of history. Plato came to Communism via the Socratic concept of virtue; the first Christian communities through an expectation of the Kingdom of God; the eighteenth-century Utopians through the philosophy of natural law; and Marx and Engels through an analysis of capitalism. Similar doctrinal twists and turns have been experienced by Christianity, which has had a Platonic, Aristotelian, Kantian, Hegelian, Darwinian and now an existentialist theology. Marx has been useful to Socialism as a guide to the modern workers' movement. But the dialogue between Utopia and science in Socialism certainly did not end with him. Science changes every thirty or forty years, but Utopia lasts a long time. We therefore must begin by putting things in their proper place. Under the domination of Marxism we have ended by enshrining current gossip as dogma and making relative what should be permanent. It is high time to rid ourselves of these notions.

One of the Germans I knew in the international Communist

youth meetings held after the First World War came to see me
last year. He was a sad figure who had suffered severely at the
hands of the Nazis, and I watched him during those years
endure hardships of hunger, prison, expatriation and, even
worse, suspicion, calumny and persecution through the fault of
his comrades. After he had finished telling me of his latest
troubles, he confided to me in the voice of one who has made a
great discovery: "We ought to treat other men the way we
would like to be treated ourselves!" There was such trepidation
in his voice that I did not dare to remind him that his discovery
was already many centuries old. But was it really old? Can you
say that a truth is old the way a person or a thing is? In any case,
since the poor man had reached that truth himself, for him it
was new-born and born well. In the saddest trials of our lives we
save ourselves by having stubbornly preserved in our souls the
seed of some incorruptible certainty. This is the secret torment
of moments of submission. Saint Bernard speaks of this kind of
suffering when he talks of certain men pursued by God. Here is
his picturesque description: "They run away from Him, don't
want to know anything more about Him; but He chases them,
grabs them, bites them and devours them." It is truly terrible to
fall into His hands.

But how sad it is to understand some things only when the
first gray hairs begin to appear, and to realize that one has
wasted one's best years and energies.

February, 1942

VII

The Choice of Companions

During the last decades the number of writers who have committed suicide in various countries has reached a figure which is perhaps without precedent in earlier periods. It seems to me that most of these tragic episodes, although differing widely in external details, have a common background: what Nietzsche called the nihilism of the modern age. Have authors' trials and tribulations less importance than their books? I do not believe so. Every time I consider the more significant expressions of the sense of bewilderment, boredom and disgust produced by our times, my thoughts go not so much to the books of Heidegger, Jaspers or Sartre, as to the suicides of Esenin, Mayakovsky, Ernst Toller, Kurt Tucholsky, Stefan Zweig, Klaus Mann, Drieu La Rochelle, F. O. Matthiessen, Cesare Pavese and others less well known. What a mournful band of spirits they are, listed together this way.

Beyond the external circumstances invoked at the time to explain the desperate end of each of these talented men—persecution, exile, isolation, suffering, disease and abnormality—one has only to know what they wrote or confided to friends to find the same confession of anxiety and desperation over the difficult struggle to live, and, in the last analysis, its uselessness. Let us be on our guard against superficial explanations. Any attempt to blame these tragedies on a given political regime fails since they took place under widely differing regimes in Russia, America and Europe. Even less should we blame the pernicious influence of a pessimistic ideology, since Mayakovsky was the singer of a victorious revolution and the others, from Zweig to Pavese, were profoundly rooted in the humanistic or religious tradition of their cultures. On the contrary, it might be more appropriate to reverse the diagnosis and state that some of them probably died as the victims of wretched anxiety precisely because they excluded it from their own doctrine and art. Inhibition is more deadly than honesty. But the decadence of our time had its beginning before these tragic episodes. And it has involved not only cultivated individuals of exacerbated sensibility, but widely differing circles and institutions, including even the working classes.

Nietzsche was the first to define this decadence and, as I have mentioned, he called it nihilism, giving a sense to the word which has remained different from its sense in Turgenev's celebrated novel. Subsequent wars and revolutions have fulfilled Nietzsche's prophecies, making visible what may have been hidden in his time. What is it about? In its most common moral aspect, nihilism is the identification of the good, the just and the true with one's own interest. Nihilism is the deep conviction that there is no objective reality behind faiths and doctrines and that the only thing that counts is success. It is nihilistic to make sacrifices for a cause one doesn't actually believe in although one pretends to. It is nihilistic to exalt courage and heroism independently of the cause they serve— here nihilism equates the martyr with the mercenary. Even freedom can be nihilistic, if it is not at the service of life but is turned into slavery, working for nothing except suicide and crime like some of the heroes of Dostoyevsky. And so forth.

How have we been reduced to such a state? We know that it is common to accuse the First World War of having been the cause and origin of much disaster. But we might well ask ourselves whether the war would have broken out if the world had not been already in crisis. The Great War simply revealed the fragility of the myths about progress on which capitalistic society was based. Even in the victorious countries the old institutions were shaken by the ordeals they experienced, and were exposed as rotten. From them skepticism and corruption descended to the bases of society. Traditional religious and moral values, which had been unwisely invoked to shore up threatened interests, were compromised in the process.

The authoritarian restoration carried out in those years, first in Italy and the Balkans and then in Germany and elsewhere, was a cure which only aggravated the illness. Where did the conservatives ever get the idea that nihilism can be overcome by any kind of political tyranny? Fascism in its various forms meant, on the contrary, the elevation of nihilism to power. Dictatorship strengthened the old instruments of coercion and created others, but it did not, nor could it, create a new moral order. And with its climate of rhetoric, fear and servility, it brought about an aggravation and acceleration of the general moral decadence. In a word, Fascism deluded itself that it was purging the Italians of their skepticism with strong medicine. And in a period when, as you may recall, hats were going out of fashion among the young, they tried to impose an imperial Roman helmet. Thus was inaugurated a public life bristling with heroic sentiments, but lacking any roots in the people's consciences. The result was a noisy, wild-gestured expression of ambiguous, make-believe emotions. Of course, it is true that the half-tragic, half-farcical character of Fascism facilitated its downfall, but it also created the unfortunate illusion that the moral infection of nihilism had disappeared along with it. Instead, its seeds were planted in people's consciences. And so in many ways we are just where we were before. Without doubt some things have changed, and among those the one we are most able to appreciate now is certainly the freedom to speak publicly of man's moral situation without having to pay lip service to a false optimism. But what about the rest of it?

Regimes come and go, but evil actions remain. The great difficulty is that nihilism is not an ideology, is not legislatable, is not something to be taken up in school, is not a different way of greeting one's friend or the obligation to use one pronoun rather than another. It is a condition of the spirit which is judged dangerous only by people who are immune to it or who have been cured of it. But most people are not even aware of it, since they think it is an entirely natural way of existence. "Things have always been that way," they say, "and always will be."

Post-Nietzschean and existentialist literature has portrayed for us man's well-known present predicament. It can be reduced to this: every tie between man's existence and his essence has been broken. Existence is bereft of every meaning which transcends it. The human is reduced to mere animal energy.

Before affirming my belief that this view is a temporary and fleeting one, I am forced to give it praise, at least from one standpoint. The reasons? One cannot, I think, help admiring sincerity, especially if it calls for a certain courage, because without sincerity there is neither morality nor art. And with things reduced to their present state, as a writer I see no other way except through the freedom of art to put before men's minds problems which otherwise would escape them and to make them aware of an image of themselves more complex than what they see every day in the mirror. One should therefore not be surprised that graphic artists have stopped representing reality as something which reveals itself as mere appearances and to save themselves have created a separate world of pure form. But the result? Their abstractions have added a new aspect to the nihilist image of the time, and the best of them have become jugglers of nothingness.

It is therefore evident that neither literature nor the graphic arts can find a stable base in the nihilist situation.

How can we get out of it? I see one way out: to explore the whole problem courageously. Even if the undertaking is loaded with risks, this problem is not insurmountable, and whoever ventures into it with absolute intellectual integrity and a sound heart is bound to achieve his goal sooner or later. There he will be rudely confronted with the suicide's coffin, or he will rediscover some valid feeling for humanity. This is no abstract hypothesis, since it is what has happened to some, and the examples are not without meaning.

The parabola of the literary work of Ernst Jünger and Albert Camus is well known. The limits of nihilism were reached by the German writer in his famous message *Der Arbeiter (The Worker)*, in which he delineated the protagonist generated by the modern situation as a new type of depersonalized, standardized, brainless, heartless and soulless proletariat, a true living robot. According to Jünger, this creature's greatest freedom would consist in the use made of it in the succession of civil and imperialist wars upon which we have already entered and which will dominate the next few centuries. "To sacrifice oneself for a faith," wrote Jünger, "means to attain one's maximum, regardless of whether that faith embraces truth or error. For in the very act of throwing oneself into the struggle, even though one is nothing but a knot of fear which no discipline and no love of country can subdue, like a martyr one bears witness to a superhuman reality which is both within and beyond one." The heroic acts of his proletarian robots would therefore be the more sublime the more they were carried out outside the traditional sphere of the human, approaching the state of the most perfected machines. This is an extreme beyond which it is impossible to proceed. One must record to his credit that Ernst Jünger retreated from it while Hitler was still in power. In his succeeding works, among which one may mention *Of Sadness,* the novel *On the Marble Cliff* and his diary of the French campaign in the Second World War, his condemnation of nihilism becomes more and more explicit and humanely motivated.

The case of Albert Camus is different but analogous. Rereading his books one can easily discern the clear line of demarcation which separates works such as *The Myth of Sisyphus* and the novel *The Stranger* on the one hand, and the novel *The Plague* and the volume of essays *The Rebel* on the other. In the *Myth of Sisyphus,* Camus has raised the topic of suicide at the beginning of the book in order to extract an answer on the meaning of life. The reasons for living are frankly defined as farcical. "Dying voluntarily," he wrote, "implies that you have recognized, even instinctively, the ridiculous character of that habit, the absence of any profound reason for living, the insane character of that daily agitation, and the uselessness of suffering." To kill oneself means "to confess simply that it isn't worth it," and affirms the uselessness and absurdity of daily life. The antidote to this lonely sense of the absurd is offered by compassion. "The world in which we live disgusts me," wrote Camus in *The Rebel,* "but I feel a solidarity with the men who suffer in it." The existence of the characters in his next novel, *The Plague,* is no longer an impassive acceptance of arbitrary and senseless facts, but a compassionate encounter of human beings who suffer and struggle against a common fate. At one point in the novel, Dr. Rieux meets Grand, a town clerk, who has been abandoned without rancor by his wife.

. . . he has just caught sight of Grand some distance away, his face glued to a shop-window full of crudely carved wooden toys. Tears were steadily flowing down the old fellow's cheeks, and they wrung the doctor's heart, for he could understand them, and he felt his own tears welling up in sympathy. A picture rose before him of that scene of long ago—the youngster standing in front of another shop-window, like this one dressed for Christmas, and Jeanne turning toward him in a sudden access of emotion and saying how happy she was. He could guess that through the mists of the past years, from the depth of his fond despair, Jeanne's young voice was rising, echoing in Grand's ears. And he knew, also, what the old man was thinking as his tears flowed, and he, Rieux, thought it too: that a loveless world is a dead world, and always there comes an hour when one is weary of prisons, of one's work, and of devotion to duty, and all one craves for is a loved face, the warmth and wonder of a loving heart. . . . At this moment he suffered with Grand's sorrow, and what filled his breast was the passionate indignation we feel when confronted by the anguish all men share.

Camus has taught us that even a revolt which is based on simple compassion can restore meaning to life.

The case of André Malraux is more unusual because that French follower of Nietzsche has shifted from Communism to Gaulism, giving the impression that he has stayed Nietzschean throughout. His stormy career seems, in fact, to be the adventure of a superman in search of tests and opportunities for his own exaltation. But it would be unjust to judge it as an external adventure, as if it had been lived by a movie hero. From *Tentation de l'Occident* to *Psychologie de l'art* we observe more than a mere change of scenery. In 1926 Malraux was announcing the historical failure of Europe, "this cemetery where only dead conquerors sleep." At that time the Communist revolt of the colored peoples seemed to offer him an adequate perspective, but his allegiance was quite ambiguous. In the pages of *La Condition humaine* a virile feeling for a new brotherhood alternates with an intoxication with pure action. In a firmer tone, this brotherhood was invoked in *Temps du mépris* as the last resort against nihilist desperation. Here we had an active solidarity, consecrated by sacrifice, culminating in the act of the unknown comrade who saved the Communist chief Kassner from Nazi torture. But had he acted on his own or was he obeying orders from above? And can brotherhood be founded otherwise than on freedom and personal responsibility? "Economic servitude is hard," the old Alvear was to say in *L'Espoir*, "but if we have to reinforce political, religious or police slavery to destroy it, what good is that?" Revolutions, like trees, are recognized by their fruits, and not by the efforts they cost.

I know that these are isolated examples and that a single swallow does not make a summer, but they serve to point to a way out of nihilism which is based on a certain force in man which can be recognized in one's fellow men.

In general the acid test will not be found in books and commentaries on them, but in encounters with other men. It has happened to many of us that we stopped going to Mass one Sunday, not because the dogmas suddenly seemed false, but because the people who went bored us, while we were attracted

by those who stayed away. The revolt of a young man against
tradition is a frequent occurrence in all times and all countries,
and it rarely happens without at least some ambiguity. Depending on circumstances, the revolt may lead to the Foreign
Legion, gangsterism, the film world or political extremism.
What defined my revolt was the choice of companions. Outside
the church in my village were the peasants. It was not their
psychology that attracted me, but their condition. Once the
choice has been made, as experience teaches us, what follows is
not very original. Almost always one accepts the language,
symbols, administrative norms, discipline, tactics, program and
doctrine of the party of one's new companions without any
resistance, on the contrary with the well-known fervor of the
novice.

It should be no surprise if the elements of the catechism and
those of the schoolbooks for the most part constitute no serious
obstacle to the new orthodoxy. There is no need even to refute
them, since the dogmas of the catechism and the ideas in the
scholastic manuals are part of the world which is being abandoned. They are neither true nor false; they are "bourgeois,"
dead leaves. The choice is an emotional one, unrelated to logic.
The fact that the new, widely accepted orthodoxy insists on its
scientific and objective character is not the least of the inconsis-
tencies which one would seek in vain in the critical consciousness of the convert. That is the rule. I have read a certain
number of biographies of anarchists, Socialists, Communists and
Fascists, and I am more or less informed about the circumstances which led certain of my acquaintances to political activ-
ism. I have yet to find a single exception to this rule. If
exceptions exist, they must be rare. In other words, we declare
ourselves subversives or conservatives for reasons which we carry
in ourselves, often in very vague terms. Before we choose, we are
chosen, without knowing it. One usually learns the new ideology later in the party schools, after having already embraced it
in an act of faith. The opposite process, that of eventual
abjuration, occurs in a similar way. Then the ideology is sub-

jected to the same brusque treatment previously meted out to the catechism and patriotic stories.

But we cannot give up our quest for understanding. What could the farm workers of his native village tell a young student in the years immediately preceding the First World War that would result in his taking up their cause?

He could not really have been thinking of a political career; and on the other hand he was unfamiliar with the proud prophecy of Marx, who greeted the proletariat as the legitimate heirs of modern philosophy. He was not aware that after the five-day uprising in Milan in 1848 Carlo Cattaneo had announced the indissoluble union of the proletariat and liberty, destined like horse and rider to gallop together through the new age. He had as yet no idea of Rosa Luxemburg's theory of the natural revolutionary spontaneity of the workers, nor of Lenin's theory of the driving forces of progress in modern society; nor was he acquainted with Sorel or the other prophets of the new Leviathan. But if the new revolutionary theories about the historical mission of the proletariat had not reached that remote part of southern Italy, it was in those years that the first leagues of resistance, inspired principally by workers who had come back from the Western Hemisphere, had arisen among the poor farmers, arousing unspeakable fear and alarm. No wonder that this unusual turmoil witnessed by a young man already disgusted with the local scene brought about a profound change in his soul, the conviction that in an old, exhausted and bored society like that one the poor represented life's last hope, a reality with which it would be salutary to make allegiance.

Those were the last years of a period when numerous facts seemed to confirm the validity of the myth that the proletariat had a liberating mission. The fascination of that myth far exceeded that of the limited programs of party politics. The workers' movement as a whole seemed to the more sensitive intellectuals to be the great popular alternative to the nihilist decadence enunciated by Nietzsche; it was the promise of a new epoch. Morality, art and ideas were directly influenced by it.

And the events of the day seemed to prove that Rosa Luxemburg was literally right. There was no risk of being proven wrong, in those years, if one stated that wherever a workers' organization was active, in whatever regime, climate or social condition, whatever its shortcomings and whoever might be leading it—Socialists, anarchists or syndicalists—it would move "naturally" in the direction of freedom and renewal.

There was one episode which became classic in the history of the movement, which seemed created solely to demonstrate to the skeptics that Rosa Luxemburg's theory was correct. Around 1905 in Moscow, the *Ocrana*, the Czarist secret police, had taken the initiative in establishing a workers' union, to attract clandestine agitators so that it could arrest them. But the agitators saw the trap and stayed away. However, the union, though founded by the police, was composed of members of the proletariat, and spontaneously developed into a revolutionary organization so that the *Ocrana* was soon obliged to dissolve it.

But we all know now that the myth about the liberating spontaneity of the proletariat has vanished since then, along with the one about the inevitability of progress. The recent experience of the Nazi, Salazarian, Peronist and more reformist and corporative unions has finally persuaded even those who were reluctant to admit it, assuming that totalitarian degeneration was characteristic of Communism alone. The collapse of that myth now constitutes an undeniable fact for anyone who takes the trouble to inform himself about the real conditions of our world.

It is no longer a question of a small group of privileged workers (the so-called "proletarian aristocracy" of the imperialist countries, created by the exploitation of colonial peoples), nor of inferior groups on the margins of the productive process (the so-called *Lumpenproletariat*), but of the normal mass of all workers. An experiment like the one of the *Ocrana* in 1905 would not be inevitably condemned to failure today. The event has this obvious meaning for Marxists: in a workers' organization the same way of living no longer means an identical or even a similar way of thinking. Class consciousness is no longer a natural product of class.

From the time this situation arose, because of which there is no longer worldwide agreement on fundamental problems, or a unanimous drive toward freedom among workers, a new dimension, not only in political life but in spiritual life, has been the consequence. The world of the workers has been split spiritually, and it is polyvalent. Carlo Cattaneo's horse has thrown its rider and returned to the wild. A worker, as has been and can be seen, can be an activist in the most opposite causes; he can be a Black Shirt or a partisan, hangman or victim, or in rich and peaceful countries simply a lazy philistine without ideals, insured against unemployment, old age, sickness and even the danger that the insurance companies will go bankrupt. But usually, in countries like Italy, because of his relative naïveté the worker can easily become prey to opposite extremes. He can still be Christ, the poor Christ who takes on the sins of others and sacrifices Himself for everyone, and he can also be Barabbas, an ignoble totalitarian Barabbas who tramples on everything in his fellow man that is most human. But he continues to be the protagonist. He is the *deus ex machina* of modern politics. It would be naïve to suppose that one could abolish this balance of powers, stupid to believe that a democracy can long survive against the workers by the use of police force and kangaroo courts. Because of their position in the productive process, their number, their greater compactness and social homogeneity, the orientation they assume in any country constitutes the decisive factor in politics. There is none stronger; man's freedom depends on it, and everything else. But since it is no longer the class but conscience which decides, we are back where we started. The choice we are faced with is twofold: it is a choice of class and of conscience within the class.

To what state have consciences been reduced? One need but look around. Many respectable people can go without food to reduce, but not to feed a starving man. Nihilism has spread from the upper classes over the surface of the whole social structure. The epidemic has not spared the lower-class neighborhood. The nihilistic cult of force and success is today universal. Nihilist is the prevalent tendency to identify history with the conquerors, as is the ignoble cowardice which leads intellectuals to Communism or to the extreme right. Are the dead and the weak always wrong? Was Mazzini wrong? Was Trotsky wrong because he was defeated? Were Gobetti or Matteotti wrong? And was Gramsci only right after April, 1945? Will he cease to be right if his party loses strength? And is the fear of the hydrogen bomb the fear of a superior reason, a more convincing reason than the others?

The universal insecurity corresponds to the individual's frantic search for protection in one of the mass parties, and this does not exclude membership in the opposition party, which may be on top tomorrow. If ideological criticism and moral campaigns do not shake the unity of mass parties and leave most of their members indifferent, this is mostly for the reasons already given. Those who join out of ideological conviction are very rare. This opportunistic inclination of individuals, obsessed with their own security and that of their families, is reflected in the usurping tendency of collective bodies. To tell the truth, I could not name a collective body today which is free from the leprosy of nihilism. It could even be said that social existence creates a climate favorable to the incubation of its germs. How monotonous human stupidity is! The deadly mechanism is always the same: every group or institution rises through the defense of an ideal, but on the way it identifies itself with and then substitutes itself for that ideal, putting its own interests above all values. "He who harms the party is against history." And for reasons already commented upon, members of the party find themselves not at all inconvenienced by this attitude. On the contrary, the benefits derived from it are enormous, for the abdication from personal responsibility thereby becomes total. If for some strange reason any doubt should arise, the doubter has only to visit the propaganda office. How many are aware that the tyranny of means over ends means the natural death of the most noble of ends? And that the reduction of man to an instrument or to raw material makes a cheap mystification of any desire to assure man's happiness? There is no more melancholy a picture than that of ex-persecutees who in their turn have become persecutors. I do not know if you are familiar with the terrible letter which Simone Weil wrote to Bernanos in the spring of 1938. It was about the Spanish Civil War. The sorrowful confession of the young revolutionary intellectual, a volunteer on the Republican side, contrasts with the vehement indictment by the Monarchist and Catholic author of the excesses of the repression by the anti-Franco forces on the island of Majorca. The letter expresses the horror of a sensitive young woman at the useless slaughter which accompanied these events; but she had seen something which left on her an even more dreadful impression than the brutal violence. It would be hard to find a more pure and disinterested witness, or a more characteristic event. She wrote:

Neither among the Spaniards nor among the French who have come here to fight or simply to wander about (and the latter were often gloomy, inoffensive intellectuals), have I heard anyone express, even in private, any revulsion, disgust or disapproval of this blood so uselessly shed. You talk about fear; yes, fear was partially responsible for these killings; but where I was I did not find that it was as important as you said it was. At dinner with friends, apparently brave men described with a friendly smile how they had killed priests or "fascists," a word which can mean almost anything. I had a feeling that when the temporal and spiritual authorities have placed a group of human beings outside the category of those on whose lives no price can be put, then there is nothing more natural than that men will kill them; when they know that they can kill with no risk of punishment or blame, they will kill. Or at least they will smile encouragingly at those who do. If at first they feel a little disgust, they hide and repress it, for fear of showing a lack of virility. There is an impulse here, an intoxication, which is impossible to resist without a degree of will power which must be exceptional since I have found no one who possesses it. On the contrary, I have found peaceful Frenchmen, whom I had not previously despised, who would never by themselves have thought of going out to kill, who immersed themselves with obvious pleasure in that atmosphere impregnated with blood. An atmosphere like that makes one lose sight of what the fighting is all about, since you cannot express that objective except in terms of the public good, the good of mankind, and mankind has no value.

The letter ended: "You go as a volunteer with the idea of sacrifice, and are caught up in a war of mercenaries, practicing the utmost cruelties."

Of course, there was no lack of imbeciles who considered Simone Weil's letter defeatist, but defeat had preceded it, as the illness precedes the diagnosis. In this universal moral shipwreck, what piece of driftwood can one cling to to avoid drowning? Among the thoughts of Simone Weil, gathered together under the title *La Pesanteur et la grâce,* this indirect answer can be read, which far transcends politics: "But we must have formed a conception of equilibrium and be ever ready to change sides like justice, 'that fugitive from the camp of conquerors.' "

Certainly we are far from the simple situation in which we revolt against the family circle. The proletarians of this world are no longer in agreement among themselves. They no longer embody a myth, and in following them no matter where and no matter what, one runs the risk of ending up where one least wants to be. That, I repeat, is why a further choice is necessary after the initial one.

To judge men, it is not enough to see whether they have calluses on their hands; you have to look them in the eyes. There is no mistaking the look of Cain. Are we on the side of those sentenced to forced labor or on the side of their guards? This is a dilemma one cannot escape since the executioners themselves force it on us. "Are you with us or against us?" they intimate. We must call bread bread and wine wine. We certainly have no intention of sacrificing the poor to freedom, nor freedom to the poor, or, more precisely, to the usurping bureaucrats who have elevated themselves at the poor's expense.

Loyalty to men persecuted for their love of liberty and justice involves one's personal honor. It defines things more clearly than any abstract programmatic formula. In this half-light, it seems to me that this must be the true test.

This should be enough to explain why literary or philosophical humanism in general has very little to say to us. Perhaps a time will come when it is more pertinent, but for the present we feel very far from the serene harmony that it portrays. It seems to us that the complacency it implies finds little supporting evidence in our times. Actually, the man of today is in rather poor shape. An image of modern man not too far from the truth and not ololololververbalized could hardly be other than deformed, fragmented, split—in a word, tragic.

This confession of humility costs us no effort. We do not know the answers to the supreme questions about our origins and final destiny. To be honest, these traditional questions do not even interest us. We have ceased to be curious as to whether the egg or the chicken came first. It could very well be that the answer is totally commonplace. The question is outside our responsibility and, however the events took place, they were not our doing. If we happen to pass sleepless nights, it is not about this. This is the nature of our situation: the problems which monopolize our attention are those of our immediate existence and of our responsibility as modern men. Only within such limits can we satisfactorily define ourselves.

All this is to say that we feel we are neither believers nor atheists, and least of all skeptics. Quite frankly, these labels with their conventional meanings have nothing to do with us. Whoever attributes them to us only increases the ambiguity of language. An unconquerable nausea at verbalization and facile consolations restrains us from abandoning ourselves to generalizations. A respect for the sanctity of the transcendent prevents us from invoking it for no purpose and using it as a drug. It would seem to me pure blasphemy to reduce God to a "problem." And if no pride can keep us silent about our moments of loneliness and anxiety when we recall with sharp nostalgia the paternal home, with its old order, peace and security, we must add that love of truth has always prevailed over love of comfort.

In a situation in which metaphysical premises, or even merely historical ones, seem uncertain and unsure, the moral sense necessarily takes up an unusual amount of space, assuming the job of guiding the intelligence. It is true that in such circumstances it is easy to fall into an abstract and perhaps foolishly ambitious moralism, but that happens only if the moral sense operates in a vacuum, as if the individual consciousness were a *tabula rasa*. In reality, however, beyond any such clear consciousness there is always the man of flesh and blood, the man of a particular place, belonging to a definite class. As far as we, as Exes, are concerned, the vital resource which saves us from the extremes of nihilism is easily identified; for the emotional impulse which dictated our initial choice is not at all exhausted by disillusionment. Ours is no isolated case. Nor is the "we" here simply an expansion of the "I." Our number is a growing legion, the legion of refugees from the International. Indeed, there are many of us, outside all parties and all churches, who carry these burning stigmata in secret.

In spite of everything then, is there anything left?

Yes, there are some unshakable certainties. These, in my belief, are Christian certainties. They seem to me to be so built into human reality that man disintegrates when he denies them. This is not enough to constitute a profession of faith, but it will do as a declaration of confidence. It is a confidence which rests on something more stable and more universal than the simple compassion of which Albert Camus speaks. It is supported by the certainty that we men are free and responsible beings; it is supported by the certainty that man has an absolute need of an opening into the reality of others; and it is supported by the certainty that spiritual communication is possible. If this is so, is it not an irrefutable proof of the brotherhood of man? This certainty also contains a rule of life. From it is born a love of the oppressed which no historical failure can put in doubt, since no vested interest is involved. Its validity does not depend on success. With these certainties which are fundamental to existence how can one resign oneself to witnessing man's potentialities snuffed out in the most humble and unfortunate? How can one consider moral a life that is deaf to this fundamental commitment?

But this must not be interpreted in a political sense as power or tyranny. To use the oppressed as a steppingstone to power and then to betray them is undoubtedly the most iniquitous of sacrileges, since they are the most defenseless of men. We must admit frankly that we have no panacea. There is no panacea for social ills. It is a lot even to possess the faith which permits us to continue. We are destined to proceed under a dark ideological sky. The ancient and serene Mediterranean sky, populated with shining constellations, is now clouded over. But the little light which survives, glowing around us, gives off at least enough light as we walk on so that we can see where to put our feet.

This is to say that the spiritual situation described above admits of neither apology nor arrogance. It is, truthfully, a makeshift. It is like an encampment of refugees in no-man's land, a camp exposed to the elements. What do you suppose refugees do from morning to night? They pass most of their time telling each other their stories. They are not very entertaining stories, but they tell them, more than anything else in an effort to understand.

That was how it seemed to Machiavelli:

Let one duty of the good man be to instruct others in that good which cannot be brought about because of the evil of the time, or bad luck, so that, among the many who are capable, some of those most beloved of Heaven can bring it to pass.

—Preface to the *Second Book of Discourses on the First Decade of Titus Livius*

May, 1954

VIII

The Lesson of Budapest

I have been told that all gift packages sent to the Hungarians from Poland in the last few days have a curious stamp: Picasso's dove weeping tears of blood. The Poles have also stolen another work of that artist. After the tragic November 4, when the Russian tanks intervened against the workers of Budapest, gigantic reproductions of Picasso's *The Korean War* were displayed on Warsaw streets, mounted on sawhorses. By an association of ideas, this news reminded me of something Jean-Paul Sartre told me. During his last trip to Moscow, when he was an official guest and was wined and dined by the highest proponents of culture, he learned from certain students in the humanities that some of his philosophical works, strictly forbidden by Soviet censorship, were nevertheless circulating in secret.

And so, when it is necessary, although an author remains silent, it is his work which acts in his stead. How sad it is, however, for these men constrained by expediency to live apart from their own creations.

Once again the intellectual Communist rebels in Poland and Hungary have not received that unwavering, public support which they have requested from their reverend spiritual masters in the West. But why should they? As to orientation and clarity of ideas, since they have already gone through more devastating experiences, they should not have expected anything of the sort.

Everything that François Fejtö told us and which was confirmed in the last few weeks by some of his friends about the rapid ideological evolution of the Communist intellectuals leaves no further room for doubt. But this is something that happens in all true revolutions. They speed up the movement of time and ideas to a dizzying pace. Budapest in two weeks has gone through the February, October and July revolutions. During these terrible weeks the world has watched stunned as all the revolutionary ideas from Blanqui to Sorel, even the most banal, were repeated.

The history of Socialist ideas and methods could be set forth just by relating in great detail the contradictory experiences of this popular upheaval. Unity of time and place, which was considered an artificial expedient of classic tragedy, has overhung the passage of events. The Winter Palace, Kronstadt and Barcelona have succeeded one another on the banks of the Danube with the speed of the extras put out by the mass-circulation newspapers. To the credit of the Hungarian Communist writers, one must recognize that they did not allow themselves to be surprised by the events. They had foreseen them; they had even announced them; and they greeted them as they would a tragic necessity. When the moment came, they did not hesitate for a minute in choosing between the party and the people, between ideology and truth. It is almost incredible. What an example and what a lesson for us all!

I know the explanation given by the old Communist dramatist Julius Hay to a friend of mine who went to see him. Actually, I had remembered him, from the days of our common exile in Zurich, as a rather strict Stalinist; but his confession will do for the others as well:

Many things contributed to my development. The first, I must recognize, is a simple question of taste. Like all writers and artists, I too have suffered from the bad taste of Stalinism in cultural and aesthetic matters. Another reason has been my direct knowledge of a permanent injustice in our society. I was also surprised at the obvious bankruptcy of an economic system which should have shown its superiority over every other, according to the official statements, but which actually brought the country to ruin. The fourth factor, perhaps the determining one, was the attitude of the young people. Because, if it is true that writers have been at the forefront—which is an old Hungarian tradition of which we Hungarians are proud—I readily admit that as far as I am concerned it was not I who aroused the young with the ideal of freedom. It was the young people who aroused me.

For many years, I have lectured. I have spoken to the students and the young workers in public meetings and at their clubs, and I always got the sad impression that my arguments did not have enough force to convince them and that they were taken for a lot of hot air.

Finally, I began to speak more freely about the bureaucracy's abuses and the deviations from Socialism in our own country. The more I exercised my critical faculties, the more I felt myself carried along on an irresistible wave of sympathy from my young listeners. Actually, our young people thirsted after freedom, and we writers had finally understood. Our situation was best described by that poet of ours who said: "I was too tired to remain dishonest."

It evidently requires less effort on the part of the Communists and self-styled progressives in the West. In our countries, dishonesty is more convenient. For this reason, I greatly appreciated the protests inspired by the events in Hungary among some personalities of the French left who are considered progressive. I was particularly disturbed by the sincere loyalty of Louis de Villefosse, who wrote with complete frankness about some trials in which he had testified in favor of the Communists: "Believing that I was fighting calumny, I defended oppression."

But how can one hide one's dissatisfaction with other statements which are noisier, but less explicit? I wonder precisely to whom Sartre feels committed, since he poses as a master of *engagement*. With his attack on Khrushchev for having revealed some "truths at the wrong moment" in his famous secret report to the Twentieth Congress, Sartre has revealed an unsuspected talent, worthy of a Polonius. Would he have the truth fed to the people in an eyedropper? Does he set so much store by public order? Would he like to issue a new version of

Machiavelli's *Prince* for the use of the new tyrants? I must confess that I no longer understand Sartre's antireformism when he says the people cannot tolerate the truth unless a certain standard of living has been reached. Does he believe, like the ancient idealistic philosophers, in the independence of economic life from the rest of human reality? But even economics needs truth, at least as much as the teaching of philosophy. Not all economic considerations, especially in agriculture, are foreign to the political decisions of the Twentieth Congress of the Russian Communist Party, just as the request for the publication of the figures for Hungarian trade with Russia has become one of the demands of the Hungarian revolutionary movement. How can Sartre persist in the false portrayal of a Hungarian proletariat as primitive, crude and selfish, and without political education, after their splendid behavior in the last weeks, and especially after the general strikes which immediately followed the armed conflict? We already knew of workers' revolts which were preceded or accompanied by general strikes, but this was the first time in the whole history of the Socialist movement that *the very day after the repression of an armed revolt* there were repeated strikes which lasted for weeks, with the participation of the overwhelming majority of the workers. This shows beyond the shadow of a doubt that the workers in Budapest have moral and political qualities which make Sartre's portrayal of them grotesque and absurd.

It is you, then, dear progressive friends, who for years have preached the most absolute faith in Stalin and his dictatorship in the West. You have put at the service of Russian propaganda your prestige as writers, philosophers and dramatists. You have carried thousands of young intellectuals with you. And now all of a sudden you express surprise and disillusionment, without telling us how or why your excess of faith could have been possible. This at least is what one of your number, Vercors, had the frankness to confess: *"It is not true that we knew nothing."* So? No one has deceived you; you deceived yourselves.

It is not by chance, nor is it of slight importance, that in the embarrassed and confused statements of the "progressives" there is no mention of the real origin of the deception. How can they continue to tolerate the ambiguities of their ideology? I think that at this moment an exhaustive discussion of this question is a necessary mental cleansing that would be of interest to us all. I would like to indicate some of the grosser and more common deceptions.

Is there anyone who still believes that we can talk about a "peace camp" in good faith? How can one suppose that a large nation or a group of nations is immune, a priori, to every temptation to pursue power politics just because it has been built on a different social structure? What substantial difference is there between armed intervention in and the supplying of arms to other countries by the Soviet Union and the same actions by countries with traditional economic structures? To ask such a question today of the "progressives" would seem superfluous, since it is they who with the greatest insistence associate in the same attack Russian intervention in Hungary and Anglo-French intervention in Egypt. But Epinal's image of a "peace camp" remains embedded in their minds, one of the persistent characteristics of their infantile view of the world: progress, peace, harmony and truth on the one hand, decadence, war, dissolution and obscurantism on the other.

If Jaurès said that "capitalism carries war the way clouds carry storms," it was because in his time there were only capitalist states; but now we know that there can be wars between Communist states, too. States, in fact, are the entities which make war.

The worst tyranny is one of words. To really learn how to think seriously we will have to begin by putting our language in order, especially our political language. It won't be easy, believe me. For example, why the devil do they still call the Russian Army the Soviet Army? Actually the Soviets have been extinct in Russia since 1920. And the last Soviets on the face of the earth in the true sense of the word were the revolutionary councils in Hungary. They were simple, improvised and open forms of popular power in a country where the dictatorship had prevented political parties from being organized.

This means that the Russian soldiers are called "Soviet" the way the Italian *carabinieri* continue to wear uniforms which date back to the eighteenth century. Unfortunately, to be understood by everyone, we are obliged to adapt ourselves to current usage and must write, for example: "The Soviet troops against the Hungarian rebels," while respect for the truth would require us to write: "the imperialist Russian troops against the Hungarian Soviets." But we have forgotten the names of things. What luck for those who fish in muddy waters!

Similar ambiguity is found in all the remaining bits of "progressive" ideology. As with the fallacious notion of the "peace camp," so with the idea of the "classless society," in which, the argument goes, as there are no classes, there are therefore no differences in political opinion. How is it possible to flaunt such absurdities after so many fraternal massacres between rival Communist groups? Is there even one person who would dare to justify the existence in so-called Socialist countries of a one-party regime and the lack of an opposition press with the demented argument that the supposed disappearance of classes has made differences in public opinion impossible? And that where such differences do exist it is only because of unfortunate interference from the outside imperialist world? If there still are such thinkers, let them explain to us, following the Marxist line, the abuses mentioned in Khrushchev's secret report of the Twentieth Congress. In a country where only one class exists officially, what were the "class" origins of the Stalin terror, the personality cult and the violations of Socialist legality? How is it that this happy society which, because of its social homogeneity, should never have to face universal problems or political choices, has seen the destruction of the cream of its revolutionaries, the genocide of five confederated peoples, and forced-labor camps with an interned population of from twelve to fifteen million?

No one has yet explained by virtue of what mysterious divine or human law the doubts, hesitations and dissent before the choices life forces on us at every step should automatically disappear in the "fatherland of Socialism." Why should workers in the same factory be incapable of having different opinions on the same facts? What absurdity and what contempt there are in this total swallowing up of man by an economic system! As if the economy itself did not require options at every step. Obviously, this is deliberate mystification. If there were not conflicts in ideas, interests and groups, which pitted Stalin in turn against Trotsky, Zinoviev, Bukharin, Rikov and Tukhachevsky, and which later caused the destruction of Rajk, Slansky and Beria and still more recently of Rákosi and Gerö, what would be the point of all these massacres? *How can you aim at the conquest of the countries of the West if, to justify the very form of your power, you have no other arguments than ones which require the complicity or the complete stupidity of your interlocutor?* One might almost think that in the "peace camp" the leaders merely played at making war, if we had not learned from Marx that struggle is the mainspring behind all reality. Marx? Who is familiar with him any more? What I have just finished reading in Roger Garaudy, a French Communist theoretician, explaining some undeniable weaknesses of the "peace camp" ("The spirit of the old world," he writes, "encircles the Communist world . . . poisonous plants sown by the regimes of the past"), is no longer an expression of Marxism, but the cheapest kind of demonology.

We have not forgotten that at one point or another, Tito, Togliatti and Gomulka vaguely gave us to understand that the long period of Stalinist terror obviously could only be explained by defects in the "system." But none of these gentlemen, after their fear had passed, told us exactly what the defects in the methods or the apparatus were. Their perplexity is easily understood. No Communist, without breaking with the theory and practice of totalitarian ideology, can discuss whether the single party is legitimate or not. The entire "system" with all its

Byzantine pomposity weighs him down. The absurd theories of spontaneous orthodoxy and voluntary unanimity in every Socialist country are the Pillars of Hercules beyond which no Communist of any group dares to venture. Beyond lie risk and perdition. *"Hic sunt leones."* "Here are the lions." Whoever dares to cross that frontier and agrees to permit a plurality of political currents, or debate and free choice for the best solution to the problems of the new society, is no longer a Communist.

The historical importance of the recent Hungarian revolt consists of just this rejection of the totalitarian lie: Socialism, yes; single-party, obligatory unanimity, no. Titoism is passé now, and Djilas, although he is in prison, appears to be the man of tomorrow. The question of the plurality of political currents is truly the touchstone which in the future will produce a salutory discrimination among the heretics and revisionists of Communism.

The intellectuals cannot escape the problem. Can we still subordinate the search for human truth (which in spite of everything should be our greatest concern), to the interests of party, state, or class, reposing in it our complacent confidence, as if by its very nature it could not fail in its "mission"? The problem is the direct concern of all who have never separated the writer's activity from a feeling of social responsibility. As far as I am concerned, I have never been tempted by the ivory tower, even though I have been told that it has no lack of tranquillity and pleasant warmth. But the ways and, above all, the spirit of the commitment must be re-examined. Only in the last few days have I read the text of a speech by Peter Vérès to the Assembly of the Association of Hungarian Writers; and I have no disagreement with him:

> There are writers who adapt themselves. The powerful think that such writers have no other thought than to serve or adulate them, but sometimes these adulators give the tyrants certain slaps, the sound of which is heard a long way off. It is an old truth that the prisoner has more spirit than the jailor, because the prisoner is concentrating on just one thing—his freedom—while the guard has

to deal with a thousand things. For this reason, it is wise to reduce the number of prisoners, especially intelligent and thinking ones. Writers should be able to think like free men, because in this way the thought of the whole people can be completely reformed.

But the justification I consider worse is the one that Sartre has given us with his inappropriate "identifications." In his view, a writer who is really alive cannot be for anything but progress; on the other hand, progress, in the modern era, is identified with the working class, which, in turn, "is identified" with the Communist Party; the Communist Party, as everyone knows "is identified" with Soviet Russia and with the People's Republics, who of course are to be "identified" with History. An admirable panorama! A whole trade show full of natural convergences!

As in a sleight-of-hand trick, the most complex and open-ended problems are resolved or abolished. What a monstrous deception! In the first link in Sartre's chain, the identification of a class with the party, a problem is regarded as solved which even in the most favorable cases really has no solution and presents itself every day in a new guise. This goes for all the other couplings in Sartre's "identifications." These are the great simplifications which lead to dictatorship, as Jacob Burckhardt has warned us. The great simplifiers are the ones who lead to the greatest confusion. Could one possibly think of a more backward tendency? The true revolutionary spirit prefers to seek differences, not identities.

But where have these identities ended up? I believe that we can ask after them at their inventor's. If they ever existed, are they not at the bottom of the Danube, under the bridges of Budapest, guarded by Russian troops, who are called Soviet? Listen to what Julius Hay thinks about it, and he was an eyewitness:

For years I believed that ours was a Socialist regime—even with its deviations and errors—now I don't believe that any more. I do not know the name the sociologists will give to the kind of regime we have lived through, but I do know that, as far as I am concerned, the deviation was everything in this system and Socialism nothing. My opinion of the Communist Party to which I belonged for so many years? The leaders have destroyed the party. It doesn't exist any more.

Clear and concise as an epigraph.

For our intellectuals of the left, who put their trust and hopes in identities which were anything but identical, it is hard to imagine a more total "alienation." It was a cruel awakening. They thought they were marching with the youth of the world, in the vanguard of History, while actually they were nothing but flies decorating a hearse. I know from experience how hard some separations are and out of what obscure requirements of the spirit, the heretic, even at the moment of his break with orthodoxy, insists that he still has his own personal faith and an unalterable love for the common cause, and even a nostalgia to return to the place of his origins. All this is worthy of respect, sometimes of pity. But let us not delude ourselves; the democratic reform of Communism, which some people are talking about, is just a trap, and one's return to one's origins a vain dream. I must say in this connection that we Italians are astonished at the admiration the Italian Communist Party enjoys in France. Stupidities are, of course, more bearable if they are expressed in a foreign language, but really . . .

Yes, Togliatti has attended his schools, as the French say, and before he was a Stalinist he was a Bukharinite; therefore he is more pliant than Thorez. But it must not be forgotten that for many years he was one of the most docile instruments of Muscovite terror, the accomplice of the Rákosis and the Gerös in the most awful crimes in Moscow and in Spain, comparable to the liquidation of Béla Kun, Remmele and the Central Committee of the Polish Communist Party. In short, he did all he could to make Stalin forgive him for his earlier Bukharinite tendencies, and he succeeded brilliantly.

Having known the temptations of heresy and having given them up to the necessities of his career, Togliatti knows how to be cynical, pitiless and cruel, especially against intellectuals who do not allow themselves to be tamed. His intelligence is useful

chiefly in concocting alibis at the most dangerous moments
during the twists and turns of Russian policy. For this he has
shown an exceptional capacity, being the only one from the
Comintern apparatus to succeed in rescuing himself from its
numerous disasters. But his famous statements in *Nuovi Argo-
menti,* after the Khrushchev report, which Merleau-Ponty
credited to his honor, are nothing but the memory of an unpleasant gaffe. At first he believed that he was interpreting
correctly the new directives of Stalin's successors, and as usual
he devoted all his zeal to making everyone forget his Stalinism.
But he had been misinformed and had exaggerated. Rebuked
by the statement of June 30 of the Central Committee of the
Russian Communist Party, he went straight back to the ranks
and has not uttered a whisper since. In a word, he knows how to
obey his master's voice. If his language is sometimes different
from that of the French Communist Party, that is only because
Thorez is less agile. The language Togliatti employed to speak
of the Hungarian freedom fighters showed a vulgarity and
insolence unknown in Italian since the downfall of Fascism.

It is perhaps useful to recall one aspect of his congenital
ideological ambiguity. It is well known that the Italian Communist Party makes a special cult of the thought of Antonio
Gramsci, one of the founders of the party and the author of
notable and often original essays. It might seem surprising,
given the well-known poverty of Marxist studies in recent times,
that Gramsci's philosophical and literary writings have not been
translated into other languages with the assistance of the publishing houses of brother parties. What is the reason for this
curious neglect? It is very simple. The official theoreticians in
Moscow have found serious heresies in the writings of Gramsci
the Sardinian. In fact, Gramsci's conception of factory councils
and the workers' state reveals the direct influence of the ideas of
the American unionist Daniel de Leon; on the other hand, "the
philosophy of praxis," which he learned from the Socialist
reformer Rodolfo Mondolfo, is a philosophy of human activity
which leaves many doors open; and finally, his formula of the
"historical block" is a difficult nut to crack. In spite of this, but

only for reasons of national morale, Togliatti has obtained permission from Moscow for a Gramsci cult limited to the peninsula. His efforts have been rewarded by the membership in the Italian Communist Party of numerous young intellectuals who were students of Croce. The autarchic triad of the Italian Communist Party schools is formed by Marx, Lenin and Gramsci.

"It's the truth on this side of the Alps and a lie on the other." At present the fraternal parties know Gramsci's work only through his pathetic letters from prison, and Togliatti, ever faithful to the agreement, has never dared mention Gramsci in speeches or articles meant for foreign Communists. But during the two months of bewilderment which followed the publication of Khrushchev's report by the State Department, Togliatti in a report to his Central Committee referred to Gramsci as "certainly the greatest modern thinker of Western Europe." When he received opposite instructions, he had to eat his words. That's Togliatti. To repay the respect of the French "progressives," there are some in Italy who prefer Maurice Thorez.

But in spite of everything, I have no difficulty admitting that there can be men of good faith in the Communist ranks. In other words, I do not share the ingenuous idea of some of my friends that the repression of the Hungarian revolt by Russian tanks represents the supreme test which distinguishes good people from evil. But we cannot transplant our own sentiments into the minds of others. The same event does not have the same value for everyone. How many times have I hoped that it would—after the purge trials of 1936, after the Ribbentrop-Molotov pact, etc.—but my hope was always in vain. Consciences are not synchronized like traffic signals.

To make it a problem of social behavior would just mean complicating the issue: should one shake certain hands or not? But in my view the real problem is another one. We have certain responsibilities toward these Communists in good faith. When I say Communists in good faith, I think in the first place of the Russian youth and the young people in the satellite countries. There are many indicators that Russia cannot escape the awakening which is striking all Eastern Europe. Let us not forget that the new era in Russian life did not begin with the Twentieth Party Congress, but with the great strikes of slave laborers in the Vorkuta concentration camps. There is a book I would recommend to the "progressives" in crisis who need to regain their faith in mankind: Joseph Scholmer, *La grève de Vorkuta* (*The Strike at Vorkuta*, Paris, Amiot-Dumont, 1956).

The revolutionary uprisings in Poland and Hungary were probably a bitter disappointment to the Russian leaders. In spite of their desire to be realistic, they cannot judge and forecast from any point of view but that of Marxist doctrine, which unfortunately is very summary and schematic. Khrushchev's conception of coexistence was founded on the conviction that the Western world was strongly corroded by inner contradictions which doomed it to decadence and disintegration, while Russia's internal difficulties and those of the satellites were supposed to be positive symptoms of growth. The Russian leaders did not realize that the relaxation of tension had produced so wide a centrifugal movement among the satellites. In spite of this, a movement in Russia back to the Stalinist policies condemned by the Twentieth Congress is not to be anticipated. De-Stalinization, in fact, answers an urgent need of Russian society. It was not invented, but rather submitted to by the current directive class. The decisive thrust was provided by the new classes of the society who thirsted after comfort and peace. A new "freeze" after this could produce "Hungarians" within Russia itself. For the first time one can see clearly the ferments which are stirring deep in that country, especially among the youth. Some pieces in this week's *New Statesman* show that a Russian public opinion is beginning to take shape.

"Then, on the eve of the November 7 celebrations," writes the correspondent of this generally pro-Soviet journal,

there was an unexplained interruption in the sale of foreign newspapers in a number of cities and there were wild scenes at the kiosks in Leningrad when the Polish and Yugoslav papers finally arrived.

Dismay, and an anxiety which became most acute when the text of Bulganin's "rocket message" to Eden was published, were mixed with a sense of confusion for which the mystifying methods of the Tass Agency and *Pravda* were mainly to blame. Speakers at lectures on the international situation were bombarded with questions about Hungary. On several occasions their repetition of the official version angered the public so much that foreign students present were called on to answer, a role many of them undertook with zest. According to reliable sources, the discontent of rank-and-file party members at being kept in the dark was reflected in the results of elections to party committees and bureaux on the eve of the November 7 holidays.

At the same time there arrived the exciting news that groups of Russian soldiers who were present to maintain order crossed over to the side of the rebellious workers. I should think that should be more interesting than anything else to the leftist intellectuals. Perhaps this is the harbinger of an unexpected spring. How many Russian soldiers joined the rebels? The Swedish paper *Expressen* of November 4 said, on the basis of eyewitness accounts, that in the first days of the revolution there were between two and three hundred in the city of Budapest alone. On succeeding days, although the outcome of the Hungarian struggle seemed hopeless, some Russian soldiers with their tanks continued to cross over to the rebels. (See the *Observer* for November 4 and the *Neue Zürcher Zeitung* of November 8.) According to other sources, the number of Russians who joined the insurgents came to several thousand. I must confess that I attribute to episodes of this sort a far greater importance than I do to the General Assembly of the United Nations.

The Russians we have always loved are beginning to awaken: the grandsons of Herzen, Tolstoy, Bakhunin and Vera Figner; the students who distribute forbidden books according to the noble tradition of underground activity; the farmers who hide and feed those who have escaped from detention and exile. This is what is important now. No one can any longer speak of Russia as a bloc.

Hence the crisis of our time spares no country. There are no geographic frontiers of peace, liberty and truth. These frontiers are within every country and within every one of us. What, then, should we do? Julius Hay has suggested *"an offensive and defensive alliance with the truth."* I find it a good suggestion. Before we do anything else, we must reconcile ourselves with the truth and establish a direct relationship with it. We must give up all middlemen once and for all. We must give up those who tell us when to open our eyes and when to close them, and what we are supposed to think. This, perhaps, is the most important task of the intellectuals, allegedly of the left, following the Hungarian lesson. We must learn its truths from the people, even the hidden truths, and make ours known to them.

December, 1956

IX

The Painful Return

At one time, I began to get "petitions," as he called them, from the parish priest in B. As soon as I saw what they were, I threw them without regret into the wastebasket. Most of them were requests for recommendations for jobs as doormen or ushers from young farmers who were tired of working the earth. Some of them asked for any job, even a modest one even if it did not pay much money, so long as the work was indoors, preferably work you did sitting down, chiefly as compensation for the moral anguish they had suffered during the war. I imagined the parishioners, accompanied by their relatives, going into the sacristy to tell the priest what they needed, bringing some little present, according to custom, some eggs, a basket of fruit, a bit of cheese, and the priest writing me to keep them happy. And in my mind's ear, I could hear him saying the deceptive words: "He can if he wants to." And then I got a different letter from him, which was saved from the wastebasket because it began: "This isn't a petition, it's news." A certain person, so-and-so's daughter, whom I had known along with her father many years ago, but whom I had probably forgotten, was seriously ill, and he thought it his duty to write me the news. Nothing else.

The priest did not know that that letter would provoke me to leave at once. For my own reasons, I preferred to take the night train. A friend of mine whom I had told the news immediately offered to drive me in his car. But I refused, giving various pretexts and vague excuses.

Just to keep him quiet, I finally said, "You know, when I left there twenty-five years ago, I took the train. So you should understand."

"But the line was heavily damaged by the air raids and mines," my friend insisted. "Many of the wooden bridges are temporary. Along some stretches the train moves at a walk. You'd have to travel all night."

"All the better," I answered in annoyance.

During the trip I remained with my head leaning against the window for a long time. Through the glass I could see the countryside, preserved for many years like a crèche in my memory, coming toward me: the stony little fields and the dark, bare, deserted mountain. I saw the little stations appear and disappear, their doors and windows bolted, their walls falling down. In the darkness I could tell the peasant origin of the men and women in the compartment by the bitter smell. They were huddled together with their boxes, suitcases and bags full of things they had bought in the city. In front of me sat a woman with a baby on her knees, and every once in a while the baby would wake up and cry. Then the mother would open her blouse and offer her breast, and the baby would go right back to sleep. I tried to sleep, too; I tried to feel like them, like that mother and child, like an ordinary person returning weary from a long trip. In the first light of dawn, the sleepy travelers looked as if they were dying. And some of them had the frightened scowls of thieves surprised by the police, the defeated faces of the humiliated and the oppressed. When the conductor's authoritative voice drew near, they searched hastily through their pockets and bags, but soon resumed their closed, hard and mistrustful everyday faces.

In the corridor, as I was looking for a way out through the outstretched bodies of the travelers and the barricades of their luggage, someone called my name.

"Hey!" he yelled. "What the hell are you doing on this train? Going back to your Fontamara?" He was a so-called journalist, the local correspondent of a Roman newspaper, who had grown old in the pursuit of dreary provincial news.

"I'm doing just what you're doing," I said in embarrassment. "I'm traveling. Can't you see that?"

His unpleasant voice came nearer. "Exactly where is your Fontamara?" he insisted in a confidential tone that was completely uncalled for. "In your imagination? Which of our villages does it correspond to—Aielli, Ortucchio, Bisegna?"

"That's my secret," I answered, as I got off at the next station.

"Where's your suitcase?" he yelled to me from the window. "Did you forget it?"

"I'm not carrying a suitcase," I answered. "Go to hell!"

I had left without baggage. It would have seemed really ridiculous to come with suitcases like a tourist or a traveling salesman and have to call for a porter. Twenty-five years ago, when I left from that station, I had no suitcases with me. I left at night like a thief, and I never dreamed that I would be away for so many years. Lazzaro had wanted to accompany me to the station. He was the one they called the frog hunter, an old-time Socialist from a village in my part of the world.

"Don't come," I had advised him. "The police might recognize you and charge you with something. Don't leave me with a feeling of guilt about that."

"I'll just pretend I happened to be near the station," he answered. "I won't even talk to you. You'll see."

So he came down from his mountain village to the station with his donkey and his daughter. He kept a little apart and watched me in a conspiratorial sort of way. But of course we ended up talking to each other.

"Leave and forget this miserable place," he said to me. "Lucky you, you're a boy and you can still forget things."

"Lazzaro," I answered him, "I swear to you I'll not forget."

"You'll forget," he retorted with confidence. "You'll finish your studies, you'll get ahead in your career and you'll forget. You'll see. It'll be easy, more than easy."

"Lazzaro," I answered, "why are we fighting just before we separate? I swear I'll not forget!"

"I don't want to fight," he assured me. "That'd be all we need. But you'll see. You'll get someplace and you'll forget, lucky you. Believe me; I'm old enough to be your grandfather and I know more about life than you do."

I continued to deny it with tears in my eyes, trying hard not to burst out crying. And Laurina, pale and meek, who had said nothing so far, began begging her father to stop, to change the subject.

"This might be the last time you talk to each other," Laurina reproached him. "Perhaps you'll never see each other again and you want to quarrel?"

"I don't want to quarrel," the old man apologized. "That'd be all we need, now when we're going to separate. I was just saying something that seemed natural to me. I was just telling him: you'll set yourself up, you'll have a career and you'll forget."

Laurina turned to me in tears.

"You have to excuse him," she said. "Really, he likes you a lot; you don't know how much he likes you; you don't know how much he talks about you when you're not around. He likes you more than he does me, and I'm his daughter."

"Maybe," the old man agreed. "As a matter of fact, yes. I like his ideas. But what am I? A poor peasant. And he, he's an educated man. And like all educated men, he'll make his career and he'll forget about us and this unhappy land."

Laurina was standing modestly a little to one side, holding the donkey by the bridle, in the sad and resigned pose which was habitual with her.

"What do you think?" I asked her brusquely. "Do you think I'll forget you?"

"No," she answered with a blush. "I'm sure that you'll think of my father often."

"And you, too," I added.

Before I boarded the train, Laurina said in a tiny voice, "Come back soon!"

The trip was longer than I thought it was going to be, and so was my absence. Some years later, in 1930, ill and in exile in a Swiss mountain village, I believed that I did not have much longer to live, and so I began to write a story to which I gave the name *Fontamara*. I invented a village, using my bitter memories and my imagination, until I myself began to live in it. The result was a story which was rather simple, some of whose pages were frankly coarse, but because of its intense feeling and the love which animated it, it moved readers in various countries far beyond anything I had expected.

It is not easy to return to the place of one's childhood as a grown man, if one's thoughts have never broken away from it during one's absence and if one has continued to live through imaginary events there. It can even be dangerous. So I was extremely embarrassed when, some days after the press and the radio had announced my return to Italy, along with others', I had to receive a bizarre delegation of my fellow villagers in Rome. It was composed of representatives of political groups and local authorities, who came to outline a program of ceremonies to celebrate my return to my home town. Taken by surprise, I was unable to improvise any kind of little speech which might cover with banalities the shudder of horror I felt at the idea of going back—and being greeted with noisy rhetoric— to those places which for me were burdened with the saddest possible memories. The unlucky delegation therefore departed in dismay, uncertain, as I learned later, whether to attribute my uncivil refusal to extreme political intransigence or to a morbid misanthropy. At any rate, to my good fortune, no one insisted.

And then came the letter from the priest at B with the news that Laurina was ill, and the description of the wretched circumstances to which she had been reduced. The unfortunate woman refused to ask me for money, but she remembered me. I had to go.

At the square in front of the station I looked in vain for the bus which once went around the valley to B. The service had been abandoned several years ago, they told me.

"Wait here," the clerk in the post office suggested. "There's always some cart or wagon going that way. In the meantime, we can have a little chat. Are you from around here?"

At one side of the square was a large fountain, with women crowded around it. I approached, uncertain as to what to do. Their old-fashioned speech and gestures were like a balm for me. The younger women wore their kerchiefs knotted at the back of their necks, the older ones wore them with the knot under the chin. When a vessel was full, one woman helped the other to hoist it onto her head, which was protected by a pad. Even the older ones held their heads high under the weight. They walked erect so that the water would not spill. Farther off, under the shade of a tree, a mother was rocking her baby; the cradle had the form of a little ship, and its motion was like that of a ship in small waves. Then some farmers arrived at the station dressed in their Sunday best, carrying enormous suit-cases. They looked like wandering refugees.

"Did the war reach here?" I asked the post office clerk. "It doesn't look it."

"This town has been persecuted by fate," he explained. "Even the earthquake passed us by, I don't know if you know. And for that reason there was no reconstruction, no subsidy, no assistance from the government. The Germans smashed their way to there—do you see that little bridge? What would it have taken for them to come up here? Nothing!"

Suddenly I decided to continue my journey on foot; as a matter of fact, it seemed preferable to me.

"It'll take you a couple of hours," the clerk told me. "You don't know the road; it's stony and dusty."

"I'll take the short cut!" I answered in dialect.

"Ah, so you are from around here," he said in surprise.

In the valley the ancient green and yellow mosaic of the vine-yards gave way immediately to a bleaker landscape. On the desolate hills the ornaments were delicate, almost artificial in appearance, an occasional cypress or almond tree, or a crucifix erected in commemoration of some long-ago Lenten mission. As I walked along, it occurred to me that adolescence has a limited notion not only of time but of space. And how does it come about that people who have always stayed in their village at a certain age move away? It is easier, it is simpler, it is more natural, and perhaps it is more honest as well, to leave at a certain age. But when you come to think of it, what does leaving mean? How many who remained, to be buried here, sighed for far-off islands and remote cities? An obsession about emigrants is one of the town's main vices. Had I ever forgotten these people or this land? Had I ever imagined anything which did not have its beginning and its end in this place?

As I proceeded, I tried to join one year to another, to put together the various pieces of my existence, and I asked in vain whether it made any sense. I encountered a rural guard with his hunting rifle across his shoulders and some skinned frogs wrapped in willow branches under his arm.

"There used to be another frog hunter at B. His name was Lazzaro. Did you ever know him?"

"Poor man. He was in trouble as long as he lived!" he answered.

"Trouble? What sort of trouble? Trouble from you people?" I asked.

"Not from me," the suspicious guard hastened to explain.

"What kind of trouble?" I insisted.

"If you must know, he didn't know how to mind his own business. He was a poor man who had barely enough to keep himself alive. Why couldn't he have minded his own business?"

"He had a daughter, named Laurina. Did she ever get married? Does she have a family?" I asked.

"If the flies haven't already eaten her, she's alive," he joked. "Marry? Who'd ever take a poor girl like that? By the way," he said, looking at me curiously, "how do you know her?"

"We used to be friends," I answered.

And he looked at me as if I couldn't have said anything more odd. "These are funny times," he mumbled to himself. At the next crossroads we separated without saying good-bye.

At the points where the valley grew narrower it became hotter; the heat seemed to be concentrated as in a stove. Then the little road descended until it ran along a brook, and soon I came to the spot where the water fell from a stony height to form a clear, limpid pool. I used to come here often as a boy, to sit on the bank and bathe my feet in the freezing water and watch the current go by. And after a while the bank began to move away, and I with it.

When I got there, I found an old woman resting on the grass with a basketful of nuts by her side. She had such a look of abandonment and fatigue that she looked as if she had drowned and was stretched out to dry. As soon as she saw me, she sat up and adjusted her clothing. She had been to the weekly market at P, she told me, trying to sell her nuts, but no one had wanted any. This was already the third time she had carried them to market.

"But even if you were to sell them," I said, "how much would you get? Is it worth all that trouble?"

"Trouble?" she answered. "Can a woman like me, the mother of a family, complain about something being too much trouble?"

She said that she had a son sick at home. The doctor had prescribed pills for him and pills cost money. So she was trying to sell whatever she could to pay for them. For three weeks she had been trying, without success. And if her son were to die in the meantime, what would people say? They would say that it was his mother's fault. The old woman coughed, and with some effort she got up and set out on her way.

I went some of the way with her, carrying her basket.

"I can't rest too long," she said. "If I were to rest too long, all the exhaustion would come back, and I wouldn't be able to get up again. The little strength I have left would seize the opportunity to leave me. I have to get up at night, too, two or three times, because I help the baker. That's how I earn some bread. I haven't time to get sick."

After a while our ways separated, since she lived near O. We stopped briefly at the crossroads to talk.

"Did you ever know an old farmer in B?" I asked. "His name was Lazzaro and they called him the frog hunter."

"Yes, I knew him," she answered. "How they made the poor man suffer. What scorn and sarcasm and even beatings he had to put up with. He was a saint. No one could say anything bad about him, and he never did anything wrong to anyone. But he didn't understand resignation. He didn't know how to bow his head."

"You shouldn't resign yourself to contempt," I said, "or to injustice."

The woman stopped and looked at me with pity. "You poor man, are you one of them, too? My poor son, what good does it do if you can't resign yourself to the way things are?"

"And what good does it do to accept things?" I countered. "Has accepting things done you any good?"

"Certainly not," she said. "But you shouldn't keep your head too low or too high. At least for the good of your soul."

"Lazzaro had a daughter," I added. "Her name was Laurina."

"Did you know her? How did you know her?" she asked in surprise. "How hungry she's been all her life!"

. . . And there was B on the crest of the hill. The village as I remembered it seemed unchanged. There was the black cluster of houses, and there still were the empty spaces left by the houses destroyed in the earthquake thirty years before. I do not know why, but at the entrance to the village I was suddenly afraid and my heart nearly skipped a beat. I had to stop a moment just to catch my breath. I would have liked to turn and flee. But in that village the bread must have been coming out of the ovens just at that moment, for a gust of wind brought me the good smell of fresh bread, which moved and reassured me. Where was I to find Laurina? I thought I had better ask the priest, since he was the one who had sent me news of her in the first place.

A man I did not know, who looked like an old beggar, was walking in front of me, dragging his feet along the ground; at about every tenth step he would spit to his right.

"Excuse me," I said, "where does your parish priest live? The same place he always has?"

He stopped and looked at me mistrustfully. "Can you give me a match?" he asked.

I gave him a match.

"Give me another," he said.

I gave him several. Then he turned his back on me abruptly and went off in a rush down a side street, without answering my question. I caught up with him at the door of the sacristy.

"He must be from the tax collector's office," he was saying to the priest. "Hide quickly!"

The priest did not recognize me right away and invited me into the sacristy with an embarrassed gesture and a timid smile, exactly the sort of gesture to inspire compassion, just in case I really should turn out to be from the tax collector's office. But at my first words, he recognized me and was very moved. In a state of excitement and gesturing frantically, he indicated that he wanted to go out and inform the Mayor and the whole population. He was about my age, since we had been in the same grades in elementary school for some years. But he looked much older than I.

"I just happened to be here," I warned him. "I'm on my way through. I'll have to leave tonight or tomorrow."

"Didn't anybody recognize you on the way?" he asked.

"I've been away for twenty-five years," I said. "Even when I was a boy I didn't come here often. Why should anyone recognize me?"

"It was more like twenty-five centuries," he corrected me. "Exactly twenty-five centuries. I'll send for the Mayor right away!"

"Don't!" I begged him. "You must know that I've lost all taste for show. Please try to understand. The very few people around here I would have liked to see are dead."

"The village suffered a lot in the war," he went on. "Excuse me for insisting, but you should talk to the Mayor. Given your present position—don't deny it, I'm well informed—given your present position, you could do a lot of good. I've written you several times, but you never deigned to answer. Please listen to me now."

"This time I just happened to be here," I interrupted him. "Since I was traveling in this region, I suddenly thought of making a quick stop, nothing more. Therefore I would be grateful if you would tell no one that I'm here. But since I am, I'm reminded of your last letter. How's Laurina? Where does she live?"

"She died the day before yesterday," said the priest. "The poor woman has finally come to the end of her suffering."

He did not see what a blow this was to me, or pretended not to.

"We buried her yesterday," he added, "next to her father."

"Couldn't you have written me before?" I said as soon as I could speak.

"I only found out you knew her a few days ago," he answered. "How could I have guessed? After all, you're not exactly one to encourage correspondence."

There was open resentment of me in the priest's voice. I could feel it in the story he told me.

"When Lazzaro died, we knew that his daughter would soon follow. Her father was her only protection and her only support. That Laurina managed to keep going these last years has been a miracle. But I was not surprised when I was called to her bedside a few days ago. I found her surrounded by some old women of the neighborhood. Did I say bedside? That is just an expression, since the poor thing had already sold her bed and was lying on a sack of straw. 'I'm not sick,' she said, 'but I can't stand on my feet any more, and so I'm resting.' The neighbors would bring her scraps from their tables. When I got there, one of the old women asked me especially about your reluctance to come back here. I didn't know what to tell them. 'My father was right,' sighed Laurina. It tired her to talk and perhaps it pained her to say certain things. But she felt she had to. It seems that Laurina and her father went to the station with you when you left. 'You'll have a good career and forget about this Godfor-saken place,' her father said. You were indignant. 'I'll never forget you,' you said, 'never.' The innocent Laurina believed you. 'Instead . . . but it couldn't have been otherwise,' she concluded."

I could have strangled the priest for the satisfaction he showed in telling this story, but I was suddenly seized by the same anxiety I had felt at the entrance to the village and I looked around for a chair, since I was having a hard time stay-ing on my feet. Meanwhile the priest continued with his story.

" 'It could not have been otherwise,' one of the old women said. 'When a head is filled with book learning, there's no more room for what was there before.' 'Yes, yes, that's the way it's always been,' added another of them. . . ."

After a while I stopped understanding what the priest was saying. I could hear a voice, but it meant nothing to me. Per-haps he took advantage of my passivity to tell me of the town's needs all over again, about the physical and moral damage wrought by the war, and the natural desire of many in the congregation to move to the big cities, perhaps as porters or doormen. Finally, I was able to get up and I started toward the door.

The priest followed, rubbing his hands in satisfaction. The street outside was deserted.

"The town hall is this way," said the priest. "Have you forgotten?"

I tried to answer him calmly.

"I care nothing about your Mayor," I told him. "I'm going back to Rome."

1965

X

Rethinking Progress

1. The Sphinx of Affluence

Some people may find it strange that an author best known by his novels about life in depressed areas and poverty-stricken villages should now be concerned with the problems of economic and social security. In point of fact, my interest in this currently fashionable topic dates from long ago.

Critics who see me primarily as some kind of sociological or political writer, with all the limitations that such an assessment implies, have never been to my liking. For the one thing that has always truly interested me is the fate of man, his involvement in the complex machinery of the modern world, at whatever latitude or longitude. And naturally I feel myself to be everywhere on the side of man, not of the machinery. If the characters in my novels happen for the most part to be either poor peasants, or intellectuals and priests in a state of moral crisis, or political bureaucrats of conflicting persuasions, and if the background against which they move is that of a b..rren countryside, this is not due to any predilection on my part for a certain kind of local color; it is simply that that is the kind of reality I know best, that I carry, so to speak, within myself—the context in which I can most clearly perceive, stripped to its barest essentials, the human predicament of our time.

And furthermore, are not poverty and wealth, after all, correlative terms? They are like heat and cold: it is impossible to have any clear conception of the one unless by comparison with the other. But perhaps it may help to explain my standpoint if I record some personal reminiscences of how, long ago, I first became interested in the problems of prosperity, and gradually, amidst the conflicting diatribes of the pundits, evolved an opinion of my own.

Although I was born and bred in a region of Italy that, while not backward—indeed, if anything, overburdened and exhausted by its load of medieval history—was nevertheless poverty-stricken, my experience of, and earliest reflections on, the situation of man in a rich and technologically advanced society date from the very outset of my life as a writer, and have continued to keep pace with it. I refer to the period about 1930, when I embarked on my long exile in the German-speaking cantons of Switzerland and began to write *Fontamara*.

It would be hard to imagine a more glaring contrast than that between the subject matter of my first novel (the desperate poverty, the exploitation, and the revolt—or rather, awakening to a spirit of revolt—of peasants in a southern Italian village) and the social conditions of the country in which I had sought refuge: a country universally recognized as among the most advanced in Europe, one where poverty, if not completely abolished, has at any rate long since been reduced to a very marginal problem.

I felt this contrast all the more keenly when in the company of certain Swiss friends with whom the divergent conditions of our respective homelands used to provide a recurring topic of discussion. Both socially and ideologically, these friends were a mixed bunch. They included architects, doctors, artisans, Protestant clergymen. Some were deeply committed to this or that ideology, while to others, ideology of any kind was anathema. But common to all of them were certain typically Swiss qualities that usually escape the notice of the passing tourist, notably a distaste for eloquence and, in general, all those forms of idle talk that we Latins are so fond of. With a few of these friends I felt a special affinity deriving from the fact that they, like me, were just then in mourning for "the god that failed." In other words, they had hoped, as I did, that the Russian Revolution would lead to freedom, and had been disillusioned, as I had been. With certain others I shared, despite our having been born into different faiths, a somewhat iconoclastic habit of judging world events, the behavior of the ruling classes, and in fact every aspect of politics, whether secular or ecclesiastical, by the yardstick of Christian ethics. The solidarity shown by my Swiss friends toward political exiles was a logical by-product of their natural aversion to dictatorships—which aversion, however, did not in the least inhibit them from criticizing with the utmost frankness the faults of their own compatriots and their own political institutions.

So, driven by homesickness, and by a passion for politics that could find no other outlet, I began to write *Fontamara*, that story of poor southern Italian peasants in which I tried to recount the vicissitudes of the clash, at once tragic and grotesque, between their as yet semifeudal mentality and the new forms of exploitation and tyranny to which they were being subjected. And even as I was struggling to get all this down on paper, I would hear my Swiss friends denouncing, with equal ferocity, the spiritual decline of their own country. Most of the fault lay, in their view, with the inhabitants of the richer cantons. These prosperous Swiss burghers, as my friends described them to me, were mentally obtuse, devoted to the pursuit of pleasure at its most vulgar and superficial, infatuated with the gimmicks of technology, and as a result of all this, reduced to a state of utter boredom. In support of their tirades, my friends would quote the latest statistics to prove the increasing number of divorces, suicides, children born deaf (this too, it seemed, being a sign of decadence) ; they would point to the spreading vogue of psychoanalysis in all classes of society, or the mediocre caliber of politicians. Nor did labor and the working class escape their share of criticism. In particular my friends reproached the cooperative movement and the big industrial unions for concentrating their efforts on the purely selfish fight for higher wages, while remaining openly indifferent to other problems of more general concern for the working class as a whole. So in all these discussions of ours we would invariably find ourselves up against the question whether this spiritual decay or stagnation that my friends complained of was really the result of increasing collective prosperity.

Was this same sad fate in store for any country that achieved a measure of affluence?

For me too, the question was clearly one of far more than merely academic or passing interest. At the time, however, I could not allow it to distract me from what, both as a free Italian writer and a Southern European having some insight into the peculiar problems of his native region, I felt to be my duty. What meaning could all this have for people on the verge of starvation? I told myself that problems should be faced only as they arose, and that it would be some time yet before the agricultural laborers of Southern Italy had to cope with the drawbacks of the affluent society.

This argument was no mere alibi for me; I was genuinely convinced of its validity, but at the same time I could see its flaws. There were limits to what could be achieved by political action; on that score I had no illusions. To work in politics for any motive other than the pursuit of personal power must surely, I think, demand a certain measure of self-deception, of deliberately closing one's eyes to certain aspects of the truth. How can anyone really believe that a change of regime will suffice to put everything right? Yet political action, on any level beyond that of mere personal ambition, must necessarily aim at shaping the future. The revolutionary lives in a state of perpetual expectation. And so the specter-gray enigmas of the future began increasingly to haunt the pages of everything I wrote after *Fontamara*. In my second novel, *Bread and Wine*, one of the characters asks himself this question: "When we're no longer persecuted, shall we in our turn persecute others?

And if ever the time comes when we can eat our fill every day, will there be nothing left for us to do but concentrate on our digestion?"

And so this insidious problem of the relationship between collective prosperity and personal ethics remained lodged in my conscience like some kind of woodworm. It was only one facet of the attempt I was then making to assess the potentialities of Marxism as a reconstructive force, and the contrast between the Russian and the Scandinavian experiments. It was already clear as daylight to me that, in the Janus of Socialism, the brutal face of the Stalinist East was utterly repulsive; but what was one to make of that benign, optimistic smile on the other face? Wasn't it just a little bit too smug? A strict dividing line would plainly have to be drawn between what was essential in Socialism and what was merely accessory to it: a task all the more urgent because of the horrible way in which Fascism and Nazism were aping certain superficial aspects of Socialism—as, for instance, in the corporative regimentation of workers, in certain kinds of social legislation, and in the mass organization of working-class leisure.

A few years previously the Spanish philosopher Ortega y Gasset had already attempted, in his book *The Revolt of the Masses,* which has since become a classic, to clarify the ambiguities of the new situation. But what made his analysis unacceptable to many of us was the palpable fear underlying it, mingled with aristocratic disdain, at the prospect that the masses might participate in public life. Ortega's prejudice was not so much against the mass man, about whom he in any case knew very little. What he bitterly denounced was the uncultivated man, "the mediocrity who knows himself to be a mediocrity, who has the effrontery to proclaim the rights of mediocrity and to enforce them whenever he chooses." We found Ortega's attitude all the more unacceptable in that the phenomenon requiring to be elucidated was in fact not the so-called "masses," which had existed both as a reality and as a concept from time immemorial; it was the phenomenon of "massification." And "massification" could no longer be studied from the outside, since the whole of society was saturated with it, and we ourselves were in it up to our necks.

We found the same hostility to new ideas, based however on a more radical historical vision, in the Italian historian Guglielmo Ferrero, himself at the time a political exile in Switzerland, where he lived, an isolated and haughty figure, almost as an exile among exiles. To Ferrero undoubtedly goes the credit (which Italians still persistently refuse to recognize) of having begun to criticize modern mass civilization as early as the first decade of this century, in an era of widespread euphoria about the inevitability of Progress. One of his basic concepts was the difference between qualitative and quantitative civilization. In his book *Between Two Worlds,* published in 1913, he developed this idea in the imaginary conversation of a group of passengers on a luxury liner returning from America to Europe. They began by talking of America, model and prototype of an industrialized society; from there they went on to discuss the whole future of industrial civilization, and to analyze its inherent elements of dangerous instability. Ferrero defined industrial civilization as quantitative, because its dynamic impulse lies in the uncontrolled and uncontrollable development of the techniques of production. Despite the increased prosperity that it brings to many people, he saw it as a civilization without stable values, without any built-in system of checks and balances, and therefore fatally destined to end, of its own momentum, in disaster.

What my friends and I found least convincing in Ferrero's gloomy vision (which in retrospect, however, strikes one as having been much more realistic than Croce's optimism) was its blanket uniformity, and consequently the absence of any loophole or inconsistency that would admit of a different principle being voiced, let alone acted upon. We had reached a point of disillusionment at which many ideals in which we had formerly believed, foremost among them the myth of Progress, had lost all meaning for us, and we abandoned them without regret. But we still felt an instinctive revulsion against any concept that ruled out, a priori, the chance to resist or to rebel.

Since then the world has seen the industrialization of new countries and the spread of mass communications extend and enforce social conditioning on a massive scale. At the same time, the shrill voices (as they used to seem to us) of a few lone Cassandras have given way to a vast and pessimistic chorus of sociologists, all brandishing tables of comparative statistics; and a mere act of faith in mankind will not suffice to counter their pessimism. This, I feel, is the most important issue facing us today, vitally important for any understanding of the age in which we live.

Until quite recently, the notion that prosperity, and even wealth and luxury, might cease to be the privilege of the few and, through the adoption of miraculous new sources of power such as nuclear energy, be guaranteed, with minimal effort, to increasing numbers of people, seemed a kind of fantasy from the realm of science fiction. Even today, many peoples of the world are still very far from reaching such a goal, still living in squalor and destitution. But at least we do know that prosperity for all has now come within the scope of what is possible, and furthermore that, historically speaking, it has come within the range of our short-term expectations (as has its opposite, the general catastrophe of a third world war, in which no one is any longer willing to believe). In other words, politics is now everywhere subordinate to the categorical imperative of prosperity—a fact which no political party can afford to ignore. Even the leaders of what is known as the Communist world, or at least those of them who have been converted to peaceful coexistence, never lose an opportunity nowadays of promising their peoples prosperity for all within the next ten years. "Write down in your notebooks," Khrushchev told Western journalists at the beginning of the Seven-Year Plan, "that by 1970 the Soviet Union will have outstripped the United States." In his characteristically colorful style he declared to the workers of

Budapest (April 3, 1964) : "We need a good plate of goulash, we need schools, we need houses, we need the ballet. All these things help to make life better. . . ." Many people felt that from that moment onward Russia was officially relinquishing (to the benefit of Mao's China) her rights of primogeniture as the leader-state of oppressed peoples. The plate of paprika stew took its place in the realm of symbols beside the Biblical mess of pottage. But in fact the bourgeois trend in both revolutionary and reformist Socialism was already discernible long before.

Be that as it may, what concerns us now is the Soviet prediction, reiterated by Khrushchev's successors, that Russia will soon be on a par, both technologically and economically, with the most highly developed countries of the West. There can hardly now be anyone, anywhere in the world, who does not sincerely hope that they may fulfill their promise. If the near future could bring genuine prosperity to those countless millions who have endured so much and for so long, it would be a matter of rejoicing on our own behalf as well as on theirs. And a lot of spurious polemical issues could at last be dropped from the East-West diatribes.

And then what? We know that prosperity, while solving a great many problems, brings new ones in its wake. But what are they?

It is hard for the layman to unravel them, since even the pundits cannot agree about the situation in those Western countries which were the first to experience prosperity. Most of these experts seem to be frankly pessimistic, and their pessimism cannot properly be discussed without some preliminary consideration of the evidence marshaled in support of it. It is now almost a commonplace to lament that guaranteed prosperity for all has lowered the spiritual tone of society, abolished the elements of risk, encouraged laziness and indolence. The description that the pessimists give of this process can be easily summarized. All those deplorable characteristics that so often render the *nouveau riche* an object of ridicule seemed to be reproduced in nations, on a vastly magnified scale, once they attain economic well-being and security. It is as though prosperity served mainly to appease pent-up arrears of hunger for coarse and facile pleasures, as though vulgarity increased in direct proportion to income. The typical citizen of a well-fed nation is portrayed as a passive extrovert, bored and boring, constantly subjected to the pressure of artificial stimuli and unable to live without them. His memory, we are told, grows daily more feeble, and before long he becomes incapable of enduring solitude or of thinking for himself. He no longer has friends; he only has contacts. In the very age when philosophers have rediscovered the Hegelian concept of alienation, reality obligingly offers us the spectacle of human beings who have reached the last stages of personal alienation even though all their wants are satisfied.

Mechanical progress, we are told, has created machines that resemble men; and a parallel social evolution is now forging men who increasingly resemble machines. To this one might retort that conformist collective attitudes, fashions, social infatuations have existed in every phase of history. But nowadays, the pessimists argue, they are being mass-produced by industry, like any other object of everyday use. So much capital has been invested in the manufacture of consumer goods, from motorcars to phonograph records, from canned or packaged foods to ready-made clothing, that the finding of markets for them cannot be left to chance. The desires of consumers are therefore correspondingly aroused, guided, funneled to the specific product. The affluent society tends, at every level, to be run by a class of anonymous, well-paid, disciplined, efficient and docile bureaucrats.

This picture recalls the caricature that, up to a few decades ago, bourgeois liberal writers used to draw of the Socialist society of the future. Medical statistics, they prophesied, would show boredom to be responsible for more deaths than tuberculosis. If this pessimistic vision were accurate, one would be obliged to conclude that the affluent society of highly industrialized countries is moving toward a type of social order that will have all the drawbacks of Socialism without any of its hoped-for advantages.

To whatever extent this kind of analysis may be valid, one cannot accept it unreservedly. Personally I always feel an instinctive distrust when confronted with one of those sweeping assessments, inevitably culminating in a moral judgment, that someone has evolved from a statistical table in which hundreds or thousands of individual cases, superficially homogeneous but basically unrelated, have been lumped together under a single heading. All too often the interpretation of statistical data will prove to have been highly colored by some ideological preference, and any one fact can serve the pundits as a starting point from which to proceed toward diametrically opposite conclusions.

Of course I myself can hardly hope to avoid these pitfalls, even though, as I have tried to explain, my interest in the question is wholly unacademic. It was simply that, after my final break with active politics, I felt the need of beginning all over again my apprenticeship in the realities of human society. I have to admit that it has taken me a very long time; but at least I think I can say that this slowness on my part was not due to any motive of personal convenience. Like every writer who envisages the task of writing as service to his fellow men, I simply felt, both personally and on behalf of my readers, the need and urge to understand. At no stage have I felt tempted to produce any monolithic or final judgment about a reality that is so plainly contradictory and fluid. My modest contribution to the understanding of contemporary society is consequently restricted to the part of it that I know best; and I don't mean this only in a geographical sense. The same effort at understanding has constituted, I think, the underlying purpose of both my essays and my novels; the form may differ, but the same basic theme is common to them all.

2. The Pitfalls of Welfare

The first hurdle in understanding the changes that have occurred in contemporary society is a certain ambiguity of nomenclature. Even authoritative writers sometimes get confused when it comes to sorting out certain basic concepts such as the affluent society, mass civilization, and the various forms of State assistance for the needy or underprivileged. One often finds these terms (especially the term "welfare state") being used interchangeably or indiscriminately, even though the concepts they denote are both intrinsically and historically different, and require to be defined in appropriately differentiated terms, even where they coexist or overlap. In the present state of semantic muddle one gets the feeling that the idiom of even the most modern languages is not keeping pace with contemporary social phenomena.

The ideology prevailing in Christian countries had always excluded the notion of prosperity for all. Economic inequality, both of individuals and of classes, was regarded, even by the poor, not as a phase of history but as part of the natural order of things. Every age had its share of Utopian dreamers, but their prophecies were invariably dismissed with the argument that to abolish poverty would upset the whole divinely established order of the universe, as confirmed even by Christ when he sat at meat in the house of Simon the leper, in Bethany. His words, if taken literally, did indeed lend themselves to this misunderstanding. When Mary Magdalene poured the ointment of spikenard on his head, and a disciple complained of the waste, saying, "Why was not this ointment sold for three hundred pence, and given to the poor?" Jesus rebuked him, saying: "The poor always ye have with you; but me ye have not always." But one need only interpret the term "poor" as meaning "despised or rejected" (for hunger can ultimately be abolished, but not unhappiness) to restore to Christ's words their permanent validity: the priority of love ("me ye have not always") over compassion. There will always be time to pity the unfortunate, but for loving there is no time to be lost. All real love is inevitably tinged with a tragic sense of precariousness.

The narrower (and now disputed) exegesis of that Gospel episode was consistent, however, with the function of mediator traditionally held by the Church from feudal until recent times. The Church exhorted the poor to accept their fate with resignation, and the rich to perform the seven works of mercy listed in the catechism: "to feed the hungry, to give drink to the thirsty, to clothe the naked, to give shelter to pilgrims, to visit the sick, to visit the imprisoned, to bury the dead." And so, until the advent of the modern democratic state, almost all forms of relief or charitable activity remained, in Christian countries, a prerogative of the Church. In every age there arose great religious orders pledged to voluntary service in hospitals, orphanages, soup kitchens, and in homes for the indigent, the infirm, the disabled. Civil authorities rarely concerned themselves with such matters until the growth of democracy in the modern state began to require, as one of its consequences, that society as a whole should assume responsibility for these tasks, irrespective of religious differences. This new spirit of secular aid (notably exemplified in the International Red Cross) has attained, in less than a century, a remarkable record of achievement. Its culminating point now appears, given certain favorable circumstances, to be the welfare state, in which economic aid and social security are complementary to each other. But here the terminological confusion begins.

In its most advanced and complete form, the welfare state presupposes a highly developed society, with widespread economic well-being, and it is basically characterized by an economic policy of full employment and by a very extensive system of social insurance that accompanies the individual citizen, as the saying goes, from womb to tomb. On the whole, this is the type of government at present existing in the Scandinavian countries, Great Britain, Holland, Luxembourg, Western Germany, Switzerland, and Israel. To this group some would add the countries of the East European bloc, in view of the fact that totalitarian control of their national economy ensures full employment of their manpower; but even their own political leaders admit that the actual standard of living beyond the Iron Curtain is still very far removed from affluence.

In countries whose economic development does not yet allow full employment or high wages, the most usual method by which the State acquits itself of the new obligations inseparable from power consists in some form of economic aid, not to be confused with what once upon a time used to be called charity. It is not a question of giving alms, but of discharging a duty. To distinguish it from the welfare state as such, I shall call this the "social-aid State." This kind of State is currently to be found at every level of development: in countries like Italy that have already almost reached the threshold of economic and social security, as in the so-called "new" countries that have only recently emerged from colonial status. In other words, the task of helping those sectors of the population unable to provide for their own basic needs (the unemployed, the disabled and infirm, the sick, the old, and also the victims of great natural disasters such as floods, earthquakes and so on) is now an organic part of the function of the State.

This new trend in the nature of political power may be variously interpreted, according to personal preference, as an extension of the Christian ethic of charity, or of the Socialist ethic of social responsibility, or even simply as a prudent expedient for the maintenance of law and order. One thing, however, is certain: the very fact that this trend has become so widespread shows how widely felt was the need for it. Like most other phenomena of contemporary society, it began, or at any rate became generally accepted, during the First World War, with the relief measures then adopted for the benefit of the civilian population, especially for the families of men who were at the front, or had been killed in action; and it grew rapidly during the immediate postwar years of economic and political crisis. Since then the State has constantly had to intervene in order to remedy the more dangerous discrepancies arising out of the unequal distribution of wealth, and to keep the most underprivileged classes of the population at a safe distance from despair and revolt. The period between the two wars also witnessed the growth of certain forms of welfare promoted by industrial firms (*e.g.,* Ford, Bata, Philips, Olivetti), which later came to be classified among the characteristic features of neo-capitalism.

Rich countries can obviously afford to spend more than others on their social services, although wherever wealth is sufficiently well distributed and society still sufficiently healthy and dynamic, it is not always necessary to have recourse to the State. Where government intervention becomes vital is in the developing countries, as soon as they get caught up in the problems of modern life—that is to say, as soon as the masses begin to emerge from their age-old lethargy and in one way or another have got to be kept quiet. This happens, be it said, no matter what the prevailing ideology. It would be mistaken to suppose that the trend to State aid is now peculiar to democratic governments, since it is also to be found in dictatorships, if nothing else as a kind of demagogic compensation for the deprivation of freedom. The basic difference between modern dictatorships and the conservative absolutist regimes of the past lies precisely in the fact that nowadays even dictatorships are in some respects forced to ape Socialism. There is nothing new in this paradox. Social services were far more extensive in Sparta than in Athens. And the three notorious *F*'s on which the Bourbon kings of Naples based their art of government (*"Feste, Farina, Forche,"* i.e., festivities, flour, and gibbets) can also be included among the many forerunners of the social-aid State.

At all events, these last decades have increasingly seen governments the world over coming to regard public welfare services as an integral part of the activities of the State. The State is no longer, as it still was at the beginning of this century, concerned merely with maintaining law and order. Today no political party, whatever its economic policy, can close its eyes to the problem of poverty. One need only reflect that the most highly developed system of public health services yet seen in Europe, that of Great Britain, was the brain child of a Liberal, Lord Beveridge (1942). After the war, in 1948, the Labour Government made legal provision that any citizen not receiving a wage or pension adequate to guarantee him or her a certain basic minimum of food, clothing and shelter was entitled to a subsidy. This law was of benefit mainly to old people, until then an almost entirely neglected category. The principle of a guaranteed subsistence minimum is now accepted by all parties in England, and the only questions hinge on the exact figure of the subsidy and of the insurance contributions.

Nor does it matter, surely, if some accept the "social-aid State" to salve their consciences, or as a lesser evil, while others accept it in a spirit of philanthropy; the significant thing is that, even within the framework of the traditional social order, economic assistance in one form or another is now recognized to be indispensable. But if everyone agrees, or anyhow pretends to agree, on this point, why does there seem to be such growing dissatisfaction with public welfare schemes?

The explanation, I think, lies in the method, or lack of method, by which these welfare schemes are generally carried out. No one now disputes the principle of social solidarity, but few people are satisfied by the manner of its application in practice. To begin with, its cost is far greater than would reasonably seem necessary. Expenditure on social welfare has rocketed out of all proportion to its results. In Italy the social security and health insurance dues paid by the public are equivalent to approximately half the total revenue of the State. No one controls, no one could possibly control, the vast new army of officials required to run these services; they seem more inclined to favoritism and corruption than civil servants of the old school—a fact which, it must be admitted, some members of the public are quick to take advantage of. Rich or poor, the citizen benefiting from welfare services is prone to become arrogant and irresponsible. Many people see nothing dishonest in stealing from the State; they feel it's like stealing from a thief. An old Italian proverb, still frequently quoted, says, "Government money is the Devil's flour."

Not least among the disasters that have befallen us in the last few decades, at least in Italy, must be reckoned, it seems to me, the widespread corruption that bureaucratic paternalism has fostered in vast sectors of the population. I have heard it said that the phenomenon is a frequent one in countries where democracy is of recent growth. Corruption finds fertile soil in the atavistic grudge that the underprivileged classes bear against everything connected with the State, indeed against everything whatsoever of a public nature. For too long, the State behaved as an enemy; from the moment it becomes dependent on public opinion, the underprivileged classes feel that at last they have a chance of getting their own back. One wonders how long this state of affairs is likely to last. The rot has even got into the framework of democratic political parties and organizations, into their trade unions and cooperatives, and it remains ingrained even after the formerly underprivileged have become relatively prosperous. If one did not happen to be familiar with the kind of situation in which this sort of corruption is rampant, or if one had not devoted much thought to it, one might simply ascribe it to poverty plus lack of education in democratic citizenship. Personally, however, I believe that these factors are inadequate to explain the present degeneration of civic virtue in circumstances of a kind that, both economically and culturally, are considerably less precarious than half a century ago.

Some of my boyhood memories are linked to a mutual benefit society that used to exist in my little native town. Although it had been started without any kind of official support, its financial situation was always flourishing, not only because it had a large membership, consisting mostly of farmers and artisans, and used constantly to organize entertainments and social functions to which members could bring their families, but also and above all because, when it actually came to handing out money, even in clear cases of urgent need, the society would encounter all sorts of obstacles. Chief of these, as I learned from my elders, was a peculiar kind of pride or shame that prevented many members who had been stricken, and sometimes ruined, by long periods of illness or other misfortunes, from asking for the help to which they were entitled. I can still remember listening to a discussion among the members of the executive committee as to how this stubborn shyness of the needy might be tactfully overcome. I noticed exactly the same behavior after the earthquake of 1915 that ravaged my native district of the Marsica. A few days later we began to see teams of relief workers arriving from other parts of Italy. We were deeply moved, of course, we were grateful, but we were also astounded by this entirely new, unforeseen and unforeseeable development, since the tradition handed down to us by our fathers was that, whatever catastrophe might befall, the survivors should bury their dead and manage, by themselves, as best they could. There was nothing exceptional in such an attitude at that time, and it was certainly not peculiar to my native town. Political parties were still unheard of. We had a county hospital, but it was nearly always empty. Except in cases requiring major surgery, when the doctor refused to operate in the patient's home, people were ashamed to bring their sick relatives to the hospital, even if hygienic conditions at home left much to be desired. To shirk the duty of caring for an invalid by consigning him or her to the hospital would have been looked on as a disgrace.

There is, of course, no reason to mourn the passing of such traditions. There is nothing shameful in taking advantage, when necessary, of insurance schemes or loan societies. Meanwhile, in my native district as elsewhere, living conditions have improved. Spending, even on luxuries, has increased; more people are now getting some kind of education, more books and newspapers are read; conflicting political passions ride high. Nevertheless the scramble for subsidies goes on there now quite as fiercely as anywhere else. In fact, both the parish priest and the local representatives of the various political parties seem to spend most of their time writing letters of recommendation and helping to fill up application forms for subsidies of one kind or another. A bronchial cold is enough to send people rushing to the hospital; beds there are in such demand that it is very hard to get in. And if a heavy shower should leave a puddle in front of someone's doorstep, it will rarely occur to him to fetch a broom and clean it up in a couple of minutes, as his father would have done; instead, he lodges a protest at the town hall, or writes a letter to his representative in Parliament.

No adequate study has as yet been made of the role now played by government subsidies in the ideology of the social-aid State, or of their psychological effect on the beneficiaries. To me it seems a new form of madness. One utterly lunatic episode, memorable chiefly because it surpassed all others in its crudeness, was that of the *"false marocchinate."*

It happened toward the end of the last war, in the spring of 1944, when detachments of Moroccan troops belonging to the French Army arrived in certain villages of the district known as Ciociaria, not very far south of Rome. All the women in these villages, with the exception of those who managed to get away in time and take refuge in the hills, were—to use the phrase coined on that occasion—"Moroccanized." The Moroccan troops raped them all, without distinction of age, from little girls of ten to old women of seventy.[1]

All the Italian Government could do for the unfortunate "Moroccanized" women was to give them a little financial compensation. Since rape is hardly the kind of experience that a

[1] While speaking of North Africans, I would like to add a remark on the subject of colonialism. In those same days of 1944, General Juin, Commander in Chief of the French Expeditionary Force in Italy, had an audience with the Pope. The Holy Father had a number of complaints to make to the General, one of them being the fact that nothing was done to punish the troops guilty of having wreaked such havoc among these poor women. The General explained that North African soldiers could not be punished because the French military code allowed colored troops the right to rape and plunder when invading enemy territory.

woman would normally feel inclined to boast about, it might reasonably have been expected that some of them would prefer to forgo the money rather than admit to their misfortune. And no doubt that is precisely what some of them did. But local officials were more than a little astonished to find that the reverse was also happening. They found themselves on all sides inundated with bogus applications from women claiming the wretched pittance allotted to the victims of the Moroccan troops, even though everyone knew that these particular women had had the luck, at the time of the outrage, to be elsewhere, at a safe distance from the scene.

This somewhat novel attempt to swindle the government provoked a few stray comments in the newspapers; then, whether from a mistaken conception of patriotism or a demagogic reluctance to dwell on an episode so unflattering to the poorer classes, the scandal was hushed up. I find it peculiarly disheartening that supposedly leftist politicians and journalists, while rhetorically claiming to have placed their hopes of social renewal in the common man, should in fact remain totally indifferent to such depraved forms of scrounging. At all events, the episode of the pseudo-"Moroccanized" women deserves a place in the annals of government aid as an extreme example of a pathological phenomenon that would repay further study. One is at a total loss to explain how, in a region of Italy where so-called "crimes of honor" are still frequent, women who were wives and mothers could go to the length of inventing a barefaced lie about having been raped, and furthermore induce their relatives to perjure themselves in support of this bogus claim. The usual excuse of poverty cannot be pleaded in this case, at any rate not as an immediate or conscious incentive, since the coveted grant was so very small (about five or six thousand lire) that the profit would undoubtedly have been swallowed up by lawyers' fees and all the other legal formalities that pressing the claim would have entailed. In other circumstances, moreover, these very same women would readily have sacrificed much larger sums of money to defend their reputations. Personally I am convinced that the only plausible explanation is to be found in the new type of relationship that has come to exist between the social-aid State and its citizens, as a result of which many of them lose their heads completely the moment they hear the words "government grant," irrespective of the amount of money involved and of the qualifications required, or the purpose for which it is intended.

Nowadays we are spared the sight of ragged paupers waiting for soup to be distributed at the monastery gates; but those little groups of petitioners one sees being shepherded by lawyers or party officials through the corridors of public offices are hardly a more edifying spectacle. No one would receive them, not even the lowest-grade petty clerk, if they were to venture there unaccompanied. In any case they could hardly find their way around in the labyrinth of red tape without some protection or guidance; not to mention the fact that they sometimes want this protection in order to obtain, not a right but a privilege, or perhaps even an infringement of the law.

Every political party, in Italy at least, now imitates the State by having a central relief and social guidance office, linked up with a network of provincial and county branches, as an integral part of its structure. The more enterprising members of Parliament have one duly trained secretary to deal exclusively with questions of social assistance, the card index of those receiving benefits or favors being the vote-getting basis of all election campaigns.

Only the leaders, it would seem, can afford to despise such tactics. But they have to shoulder other and more onerous tasks, on a collective scale, as when, for instance, relief must be provided for a whole sector of the population stricken by some natural catastrophe. In Italy such catastrophes are unfortunately frequent. And it must be admitted that, due partly to the general improvement in living conditions, the organization of relief, both public and private, is now increasingly speedy and effective. But even these tragic occasions have their ignominious aspects. All too often, the methods of providing relief are such as to foster a "professional victim" mentality among the survivors.

Recent testimony to this deplorable state of affairs was furnished by the Socialist mayor of a small town that was flooded and razed to the ground when the dam of an artificial lake suddenly gave way. Most of the inhabitants lost their lives. For those who survived, relief funds came pouring in swiftly and abundantly from every other province of Italy. So what did the Socialist mayor have to complain about? He complained that the methods by which these funds were distributed were utterly mistaken. The survivors, instead of being helped to get back to normal and make a new start, were dealt with in the most summary fashion, by being simply handed large sums of cash, far larger than anything they had ever been accustomed to. Such trust was misplaced, for they straightaway plunged into orgies of spending and carousing, thus bearing out the old saying, "Easy come, easy go."

"The result," said the mayor, "is that in one of the factories many of the workers, now that their pockets are full of money, have walked out of their jobs. They spend their days in idleness, sitting around for hours on end in one or the other of the numerous bars that, since the disaster, have sprung up like mushrooms; or else they wander here and there trying to collect further subsidies; and meanwhile the factory is at a standstill."

As it happened, the protagonists of this episode were not backward peasants of the underprivileged South, but skilled industrial workers of Longarone, in the northern province of Belluno, reputedly one of the most modern and progressive in the peninsula. In my view no region of Italy and no category of its population is at present uncontaminated by this lamentable degeneration of the sense of citizenship.

In fact, only a little while before the disaster of Longarone, and in almost identical circumstances, the farmers of another region, when it was flooded by the waters of the Po, behaved in identical fashion. As the level of the floodwaters continued to rise, teams of relief workers rushed from neighboring provinces —firemen, carpenters, bricklayers, under the supervision of engineers and technicians. On the stronger of the two banks of the river, at a safe distance from the flood, the women bivouacked with their children amid piles of salvaged furniture and household effects of every description, while the husbands and grown-up sons sat around café tables in the *piazza*. Why couldn't they too have pitched in, taken some part in the rescue work? Why didn't they lend a hand in reinforcing the danger points of the embankments, or evacuating the farmhouses threatened by the flood? The answer is that, since they were natives of the place and in one way or another interested parties, no one would have paid them. But they rushed to the town hall the moment word got around that clothes and blankets were going to be handed out free.

The most distressing aspect of this decadence, in my view, is not so much the loss of all spontaneous generosity, nor the continual and arrogant claiming of what is due, as the miserable pettiness of such claims. The fact that rights imply duties as their counterpart being beyond the comprehension of these unfortunate people, they remain unaware of, or indifferent to, the greatest possible right they could claim, the right to be respected as men and to conduct themselves as men, the right to be citizens and not herded cattle; instead, they will fight tooth and nail to establish their right to handouts, gift parcels, free entertainments.

The opinion I once held, namely, that social welfare could be made to work better if it were taken out of the hands of the bureaucrats and entrusted to the responsibility of those directly concerned, has been badly shaken by seeing people reduced to the plight I have just described. It is of course far easier to get away with swindling a public office than to deceive one's own workmates. But how to ensure that those elected to responsibility would really be the most honest? And how long would their honesty resist the pressures and petitions of their relatives, friends and party comrades?

3. Morality and Welfare

Underlying some of the criticisms currently voiced about the moral situation of rich countries where prosperity has reached all classes of the population, there are some historical disillusionments.

The long-awaited dawn of economic and social security has given an answer to the problem raised by the revolutionary thinkers of the nineteenth century, who claimed that the chief task of political science was to define the conditions under which man could best attain and develop his freedom. In adopting this concept, later generations of political thinkers made the mistake of forcing on it a deterministic connotation of cause and effect, thus spreading the illusion that what had been originally promulgated as a moral aim would come about automatically as a result of economic change. But the root of the error lay in the original theory.

The disillusionment to which this theory has led could hardly be more complete, since it is to be found not only in those countries where social progress has been pursued and achieved within the framework of traditional social structures and by reformist measures, but also in those where a clean sweep has been made of the past and a new regime established. But even where the reorganization of society has been most successful, the immense alleviation of human suffering brought about by science and by economic democracy has not produced a corresponding reform in the patterns of human behavior. In short, the prophets of social emancipation had reckoned without the old Adam. The fault lay, of course, not in their hopes, but in their belief that these hopes could be fully realized simply as a by-product of increased consumption or institutional changes. In reality the relationship between human freedom and the external factors conditioning it is not something that can be defined according to a hard and fast rule. One is almost tempted to say that, in an era in which the techniques of automation are being constantly perfected, the one mechanism to have broken down is that which, by abolishing poverty, ought *ipso facto* to have produced a new type of citizen, endowed with more highly developed mental and moral qualities than before.

It has begun to look as though this failure were at last being recognized even by those Western Communists who used to visit the Soviet Union in the spirit of devout Muslims on pilgrimage to Mecca, projecting their own dreams onto the harsh and merciless reality of their adopted country and returning home with the announcement that they had discovered a new type of human being. (One Italian psychoanalyst went so far as to justify the fact that both the practice and the theory of psychoanalysis were forbidden in Russia by arguing that "in a socialist country people shed their complexes automatically.") But as a result of de-Stalinization and of the ideological repercussions of Moscow's conflict with Peking, a certain degree of realism is now permitted even to the most zealously orthodox comrades. The discrepancy between dream and reality is nevertheless so wide as to frighten even the Communist revisionists, who shrink from going all the way in their critical rethinking of Communist theory for fear of shaking its foundations.

All this does not mean, of course, that the old Adam is insensible to environmental pressures; far from it. It is simply that, in many respects, he reacts to new conditions differently from what had been anticipated.

The optimistic theories about what was presumed would be man's automatic response to progress first began to break down in the relationship between science and freedom. It was thought that modern science and technology could forge rapidly ahead only in a general atmosphere of freedom; and that, reciprocally, by creating new opportunities for man's development, science and technology would then lead to even greater freedom. In fact something very different has happened: the advance made in scientific and technological research even under Hitler and Stalin proved that science could flourish without the oxygen of human liberties; and, far from endangering the stability of either the Nazi or the Soviet regime, it endowed them with new instruments of power.

Another point at which the supposed mechanism of automatic development has failed to function is the relationship between prosperity and democratic participation in public life. One of the most frequently encountered characteristics of the affluent society would appear to be a decline in the political dynamism of the masses; this can go to the point of inertia and indifference, except for short periods of electioneering when the party machines swing into action, rousing the citizen from his torpor.

Bertrand de Jouvenel, who has made a special study of these phenomena, quotes a page of Engels from *Anti-Dühring* that is of some relevance to my problem. Engels maintained that the length of the working day has a direct bearing on the interest and participation of the working classes in matters of public concern:

Up to the present day all the historical antagonisms between exploiting and exploited classes, between rulers and oppressed, were to be explained by the lack of development in the productivity of human labor. As long as those sections of the population employed in manual labor were so tied down by their basic tasks as to have no spare time for matters of general interest (labor leadership, national and local politics, juridical questions, art, science, etc.), such matters inevitably required the existence of a special class, exempt from material work, that could be exclusively responsible for them. This privileged class has never failed to take advantage of the situation by imposing a constantly heavier burden of labor on the working masses with a view to its own profit. It is only the enormous increase in production, brought about by large-scale industry, that makes it possible at last for work to be distributed fairly among all the members of society, thus cutting down the individual number of working hours so that everyone will have sufficient free time to devote to the problems, both intellectual and practical, that concern society as a whole. It is therefore only now that the existence of a ruling and exploiting class has become superfluous, or rather an obstacle to social progress. And so now at last the moment has come for it to be ruthlessly suppressed.

The logic of Engels' argument might seem flawless, but it is out of touch with reality. If a manual or a white-collar worker is to take an active part in the life of the community, he will undoubtedly need a reasonable amount of free time; but free time is not the only prerequisite, nor even, as events have already shown, the most important one. Not only has the fact that the working classes now enjoy a certain amount of leisure not sufficed to bring about the Utopian dream of giving greater social content to the creative activity of thinkers, scientists and artists, or of widening the class from which artists and intellectuals have so far been drawn; it does not even suffice to ensure that every citizen will take a livelier and more intelligent interest in his political choices and decisions. Unfortunately neither the advent of greater prosperity nor the reduction in working hours has freed any sector of political life from its oligarchical structure. This oligarchical tendency has indeed become more pronounced in recent decades, as a single fact will suffice to prove. Until about forty years ago, it would have been impossible for any political party to conceal the details of its financial report from the rank and file of its members, while now there are countries, among them the one I happen to know best, where party finances are a jealously guarded secret.

But there is also another symptom of our time that invalidates Engels' forecast, the mere diagnosis of which is, in my opinion, enough to settle the question. Not so long ago, when the working day of factory hands, clerks and agricultural laborers lasted from between ten to twelve hours, there were countries where most of the work connected with political parties, both at the local and provincial levels as well as at the top, was done by volunteers, that is to say by party members who sacrificed their Sundays and the few leisure hours that were left to them on weekday evenings. (And because there was, in those days, much less contact than there is now between politics and the economy, State intervention was less ubiquitous and party work yielded neither perquisites nor pickings.) Although today party workers in the same countries have much more leisure than before, they seem to spend most of it just hanging around in the street or square or in cafés, chatting to their friends, or else glued to the television set. There is now scarcely any kind of work connected with political parties or trades unions or cultural societies that has not got a salary attached to it. In Italy even the Communist and Christian Democrat schoolboys, if they are asked to distribute leaflets in the streets or scribble slogans on the walls, will refuse to do it unless they get paid. Such instances alone are sufficient, in my view, to show why a phenomenon so vast and so peculiar cannot be explained (as Bertrand de Jouvenel suggests in his otherwise penetrating comment on the lines he quotes from Engels) by the greater number and complexity of the problems that have arisen in our time.

It seems to me that where sociological writings about the affluent society tend most frequently to go wrong is in their false generalizations. Every country shares certain, perhaps most, things in common with others, but it has also much that is peculiar to itself. To put it crudely, it is hardly likely, for instance, that the self-made man will have much in common with the scion of a family which has been wealthy for generations, beyond the size of their bank accounts. So prosperity can have its children's diseases, its growing pains, just as the citizens of a welfare or a social-aid State may react to it in the childish manner which I have previously described. And since today Italy provides perfect examples of everything that is childish, I would like at this point to say a little more about it.

Italy has in recent years attained a rung about halfway up the ladder of economic advancement, although many people still continue to talk of it as a country where poverty not only prevails but is endemic, while others exaggerate the so-called "Italian miracle." However, one may detect a certain significance in the fact that, until quite recently, whenever the word "miracle" appeared in an Italian newspaper it invariably referred to a statue of the Virgin that had been seen to shed tears, or to a bricklayer fallen from a scaffolding and saved from certain death by the intervention of St. Anthony. Now the term "miracle" is applied to the enormous number of motorcars that have brought the traffic in the streets of Italian cities almost to a standstill, and to other indications of material prosperity. Not every region, obviously, nor every class of the population, has benefited to the same extent from the rise in the standard of living, but a curious euphoric mood of feeling suddenly rich seems to have got hold of a great many poor people simply because they no longer go barefoot, because they can eat at least two meals a day, and because coffee, which formerly they could afford only as a kind of occasional medicine, has now become their daily beverage.

The strange thing is that in order to obtain a government subsidy, on whatever pretext, people will pretend to be very poor, while elsewhere ostentatiously trying, with equal untruthfulness, to convey the impression that they are rich; but strange though this may be, it happens all the time. A good picture of this split mentality appears in a book written by Don Lorenzo Milani, priest of the parish of San Donato, near the town of Prato in Tuscany. San Donato is a small place that in recent years has achieved a certain prosperity. Don Milani described the various ways in which the peasants and working men of his parish do their utmost to ape the rich. On such festive occasions as baptisms, first communions and weddings, the poorest families will vie with each other in orgies of unnecessary and frivolous spending on printed announcement cards, hired limousines, professional photographers, printed souvenir cards, extravagant banquets for a multitude of guests—while the homes of these same people may lack the most elementary forms of plumbing.

According to Don Milani, they are equally addicted to public festivals. It takes very little organizing to make a success of any function, whether it be in honor of a local politician, a cycling champion, or the Virgin Mary, or the annual bazaar held under the auspices of the Communist daily newspaper. The crowd is more or less always the same, as is almost inevitable in a small place where everyone knows everyone else. The purpose of the celebration doesn't matter; people simply come to have a good time. Sunday is no longer the Lord's Day, if indeed it ever was that; for some years now its culminating moment has been in the late afternoon when the results of the weekly football pools are announced over the radio. And since in the summer months, when there are no football matches, Sunday threatened to become a day of boredom and desolation, the government hastened to the rescue by authorizing the organization of betting on other sporting events. Thus Sunday after Sunday renews in every heart the hope of sudden riches.

In order to compete with its chief adversary, namely, Communism, for the favor of a public grown so vulgar in its tastes, the Church has not hesitated to adopt the new techniques of entertainment that are now typical of every mass organization, such as cinemas, and amusement halls complete with bars, billiard tables, jukeboxes and pin-ball machines. In a parish not very far from that of Don Milani, three parochial bars were laid on and blessed by no less a person than the Archbishop. By resorting to such expedients, the Church may intend to stem the invasion of vulgarity; in fact, vulgarity is made respectable and all-pervading. The means devour the ends. The amusements provided become the main objective of the crowds that flock to the parochial halls.

The other side of the coin shows an identical picture. Everything that this Tuscan priest has written about the spiritual stagnation and emptiness of parish life holds good for the local branch of the Communist Party. It could hardly be otherwise. If the whole countryside is stricken by drought, the parish priest's garden and the Communist leader's vineyard are equally

blighted. To the de-Christianization of the faithful there corresponds a parallel trend in the Communist movement toward
the adoption of bourgeois ways, or at any rate a bourgeois
mentality, and toward bureaucratism. In most Italian villages,
no hard-and-fast line can be drawn between the membership of
the Church and that of the Communist Party; they overlap,
intercommunicate and to a large extent coincide. Even the
"Children of Mary"—young girls who in bygone days used to be
the exclusive preserve of the parish—now seemed inclined, at
least in the more advanced districts, to run with the hare and
hunt with the hounds. If a girl is vain about her looks, she will
go anywhere to show them off, provided there is a crowd. Don
Milani ironically calls these girls "the faithful followers." They
attend every religious ceremony, faithfully walk in every procession, faithfully turn up at every sports event, faithfully take part
in every Communist festival. They devote exactly the same
amount of time and trouble to getting themselves ready in front
of the looking glass whether they are going to a Holy Thursday
sermon or to a dance organized by the Communist daily newspaper, *L'Unità*. Nothing could induce these "faithful" girls to
give up a single sermon or Communist ball unless they happened to know in advance that the attendance was likely to be
poor. In short, they are Catholics in the same way as they are
Communists; that is to say, they are neither the one nor the
other. Both the Church and the Italian Communist Party get
what they deserve.

To describe Catholics of this sort as believers, or Communists
of this sort as atheists, is therefore an insult to both Church and
party. They are all cast in the same mold; they are all driven by
the same compulsions; they all hanker after the same things,
believe in the same values, share the same dream—to score
thirteen out of thirteen in the football pools and to become
millionaires overnight. Their chief concern, be they Catholic or
Communist, is that other people should not think them poor.
In the minds of the common people of Italy, poverty has become a disgrace, even when, as is mostly the case, the poor are

poor through no fault of their own. Anyone having witnessed a brawl in the streets of an Italian city knows that nowadays the most frightful insult conceivable, second only to disrespectful insinuations about the ancestors of one's adversary—the insult that leaves one no choice but to resort to violence—is the epithet *"Morto di fame!*—starved to death!"* (In English it might be rendered as "You penniless wretch!") Whether warranted or not, the accusation is an unpardonable one, implying as it does the announcement to the world at large that the other person is poor. Of course this does not prevent Italians, throughout the peninsula, from cultivating special devotion to St. Francis, the Poor Man of Assisi.

But to make a great show of despising poverty is not the same thing as being rich. If we want to find the typical features of a genuinely affluent society, as criticized by the sociologists, we must leave Italy and look elsewhere. Until some time ago North America used to be considered the prototype of countries in the vanguard of economic progress, and the phrase "American way of life" was thought to sum up everything that was both good and bad in an affluent society. Recently, however, a number of writers, foremost among them the French political scientist Raymond Aron, have suggested the term "industrial civilization" as more appropriate, both because it would cover certain European nations, such as Sweden (whose collective prosperity is now on a par with that of the United States), and also because it would ultimately allow Russia (a country where individual living standards still notoriously lag behind but which in other respects is recognizably following the same trend) to be included in the category. It should not be forgotten that the climax of the famous television debate between Khrushchev and Nixon in August, 1959, was not a conflict of ideals, but an argument as to which of their respective countries would succeed in producing the greater number of washing machines and ready-made garments in the course of the next few years. The subsequent break with Chinese Communism has accentuated the new trend of Russian economic policy toward the production of consumer goods. After almost half a century of enforced austerity in the service of ruthless power politics, Khrushchev rediscovered the simple truth that—to use his own words—"after all, revolutions are made so that people may live better. . . ." But now that the goal of Soviet planning is officially defined as being "to reach and surpass the American standard of living," now that the Soviet leaders justify the system of state capitalism prevailing in Russia with the final and decisive argument that, for countries that are still backward, it is the shortest cut to economic progress, sociologists and political scientists have got a common denominator and a uniform criterion for judging industrial civilization as a whole.

In short, both the American and the Soviet systems have as their common ideal a higher standard of living; and in both countries the model citizen, the pieceworker or the Stakhanovite is efficient, well fed, conventional in his ideas, law-abiding and uninterested in politics.

Certain differences do, of course, persist. A leading Soviet official doesn't own a motorcar, he only has the use of one; but there are plenty of Western bureaucrats to whom this would seem a very agreeable arrangement. If the car belongs to the State or to some other public institution, there is the advantage that the person using it doesn't have to pay for petrol or repairs. (The only one to suffer is the motorcar.) Social inequality still persists, but tends increasingly to derive from perquisites and privileges rather than from private property. One may safely predict that the status symbols of the future will consist, not in being able to afford one's own house, a retreat in the country, a yacht and several motorcars, but in being able to have all these things at one's disposal free of charge. In other words, social relations tend increasingly to be dominated by consumption rather than production; but it would be rash to assume that this development will necessarily bring about social peace and harmony. The old law of *homo homini lupus* that governed the conditions of human life in the primeval forests may well prove to be still valid even in the world of TV aerials and big department stores.

Affluence breeds its own diseases; the assertion that prosperity must result in a state of uncreativity and boredom seems to be entirely unfounded. It belongs to the same category of rhetorical clichés as that other remark one often hears about poverty being somehow conducive to a gay and productive life. Tourists may be forgiven such misapprehensions, but not sociologists. The Scandinavian arriving in a Mediterranean city may be dazed by the sun, the noise, the shouting of half-naked children in narrow and filthy lanes, the hawkers crying their wares, the conversation conducted, at the top of their voices, by two people of whom one is standing in the street and the other leaning out of a top-floor window. All this can easily give the visitor from some northern land an impression of gaiety and excitement; but such an impression would be essentially false, as false as the opposite one that Italian journalists never fail to bring back with them: the sepulchral gloom of Sunday morning in a rich Protestant city. (The origin of this alarming sensation proves, on closer examination, to be the total absence of the uproar to which Italian city-dwellers are accustomed—especially on Sundays when it explodes in a paroxysm.) And if we pass from the articles of Italian journalists to the books of certain sociologists, we might find ourselves imagining the Sabbath silence of those capitals of opulence being broken, toward evening, by the muffled sound of revolver shots: the boredom of prosperity driving its victims to suicide.

This topic of the soaring suicide rate in countries where prosperity is widespread recurs invariably in every argument about the civilization of the affluent society. I confess that I am unable to speak of it from personal experience. But a great deal has been written about it, and the opinions expressed are, fortunately, conflicting. In fact, lately an increasing number of voices have been raised to challenge the trite assertion that social security makes people bored with life. Contrary to popular belief, one finds, for instance, that the suicide rate in Sweden has remained almost constant throughout the past decades: an annual average of ten cases per hundred thousand inhabitants. In a world-wide classification this figure puts Sweden tenth among the nations, well behind Japan, Austria, Finland and other countries that are still far from having reached general prosperity. But it is easier to count the number of suicides than to ascertain their cause. How can one possibly know for certain what private despair drives a human being to take his own life? Even if every suicide wrote a detailed confession before committing the act, we would still be largely at sea. Who could guarantee that the confession was reliable or that the suicide was fully aware of his own motives? Many of the letters that these unhappy people leave behind them seem rather to suggest the epitaph that they would like to have inscribed on their tombstones.

Insofar as it is at all possible to venture, however tentatively, on the study of such an impenetrable problem, I think that the conclusions reached by an eminent American psychiatrist, Professor Herbert Hendin of Columbia University, along lines previously traced by other scholars, are extremely convincing. Professor Hendin has done a vast amount of meticulous research on a great many suicide cases in Denmark and Sweden, and was able to talk freely to a number of would-be suicides who survived their unsuccessful attempts. Professor Hendin found that the most frequent cause of despair was not boredom but its opposite: breakdown under the strain of living at too intensive a pace. It seems that the majority of Danes and Swedes are trained, at home, in school, in the army and on the sports fields, to live at the highest pitch of their capacity. Despite general prosperity, there is severe competition on every rung of the social ladder, and many people feel it is a humiliation to be outdone. Not only that, but in the sphere of private life there are the complexes and inhibitions which, according to psychoanalysts, afflict Northern peoples more than others. The latter seems to be borne out by the literature, the drama and even the films that continue to come out of Scandinavia.

4. The Two Faces of Mass Civilization

To revile television, radio and the popular press as deadly instruments of modern civilization has by now become a platitude. The sociologist engaged in the study of this subject is likely to have an experience similar to that which, according to a skit by the Roman poet Pascarella, befell Columbus and his companions when they first met a native on American soil.

They stopped and, summoning their courage, addressed him. "You, there!" they called out. "Who are you?" "Who do you think I am?" he retorted. "A savage, of course!"

Research, too, is only too liable to bag the kind of quarry for which the questioner has been laying traps all the time. This applies as much to the critics of mass civilization as to its apologists, irrespective of their good faith or intellectual qualifications.

At one of the first round-table discussions between Western and Eastern European writers held in Venice under the auspices of the *Société Européenne de Culture,* I remember an astonishing remark made by Professor J. D. Bernal, who occupies the Chair of Physics at the University of London's Birkbeck College, and is a Fellow of the Royal Society.

"In capitalist countries," said Professor Bernal, "culture suffers from the gulf that separates the common people from the higher forms of art—James Joyce, for instance, being read and understood only by a handful of initiates, while the masses are content with comic strips. On the other hand, I have seen for myself how successfully this gulf has been bridged in the socialist society of Russia, where kolkhoz workers, students, scullery hands, poets, scientists all read the same books, enjoy the same films and paintings—in short, share the same aesthetic values."

Coming as it did from a British scientist, presumably steeped in analysis and an empirical approach to things, the announcement of such a miracle should normally have left no room for doubt. But as it happened, four Soviet writers were sitting at the same table, and to let slip such an opportunity of getting this wonderful news confirmed on the spot would have been grave negligence on my part. I consequently hastened to intervene. "Without intending any disrespect to my illustrious colleague, Professor Bernal," I said, "may I ask our Soviet colleagues here to tell us how this miracle was achieved?"

The thankless task of answering my question was undertaken, after some hesitation, by the Soviet novelist, Konstantin Fedin. He spoke with commendable honesty.

"In Russia, too," he said, "we have a division of cultures; apart altogether from the higher forms of culture, in Russia, too, we produce a great many books and films which have no artistic value and are put out purely for mass consumption." The silence that followed was broken only by a few embarrassed coughs. Some people began to gaze intently at the white ceiling. The incident was too painful to invite comment. This notion of a new relationship between the Russian people and art had been a figment of Bernal's imagination, a conclusion the distinguished British scientist had arbitrarily drawn from the premises of his own political credo.[2]

But this is not really a subject that one can be facetious about. To re-create the unity of culture in the sense in which it may be said to have existed during the Christian Middle Ages when the artist and the common people were part of the same spiritual world, spoke the same language and believed in the

---

2 Professor Bernal was one of the "Western scientists" who, in the second year of the Korean War, when the Chinese were accusing the Americans of waging bacteriological warfare, certified that the charges were "scientifically" justified.

"I suppose," I said to him when we were chatting alone for a moment, "you deduced that from the incontrovertible fact that America is a capitalist country?" "No," he said, "as it happens, I analyzed a fly. . . ." "A fly?" I said. This was interesting. "No doubt you caught it yourself just as it was being dropped from an American aircraft? Was it carrying its birth certificate and its *curriculum vitae?* And why did you stop talking about bacteriological warfare the moment Chinese propaganda no longer needed it? Why do you never mention it now?"

He looked at me contemptuously with scorn in his eyes of the kind which the true believer reserves for the infidel.

same symbols, far more would be needed than a new set of bureaucrats at the levers of power or a more equitable distribution of wealth.

One ought to say here in parentheses that the orphans of Stalinism may derive consolation from the fact that the cultural gap continues to exist (as was only to be expected) even in those countries which have experienced the peaceful revolutions of Labor or Social Democracy. In all fairness we must recognize that, under both Communist and Social Democratic regimes, the working classes have made great advances; but it would be idle to pretend that new cultural values have emerged from them. Where changes in the structure of society have given working-class people freedom to enter upon literary or artistic careers, it might reasonably have been expected that a fresh wind would blow through literature and the arts; but nothing of the sort has happened.

In countries where collective prosperity is a fairly recent achievement [writes the Swedish novelist Bengt Holmqvist] one used to hear a lot of optimistic talk about the untapped reserves of talent that would now enjoy full scope and freedom to express themselves. In Sweden the combination of an almost completely elastic class structure with so many new educational opportunities has undoubtedly released an impressive flow of intellectual energy. But it looks as if the day were already past when young people of working-class origin could become members of the creative intellectual elite. Such meteoric rises in social status were a feature of the 1930s and 1940s, when the "silent revolution" was still in progress and the new society emerging from it had not yet attained stability. Those were the days of the "young proletarian writers" (as they were called) whose immediate background was one of poverty and hardship. In becoming writers they did not perhaps greatly improve their material situation, but neither did their choice require undue sacrifices; at all events it meant a rise in the social scale. Now things have changed. The writer's material situation is at best precarious, and many other openings exist for the intellectually gifted. In our flourishing "meritocracy," almost anyone can attain a position of respectability and economic security; and those who feel an irresistible urge to write can be certain of finding some outlet for it. But it is hardly fortuitous that most of the new writers to emerge in recent years should have been men and women with academic training and no illusions about the literary profession. They bring to it a kind of Alexandrian subtlety, but not very much first-hand experience of life. The proletarian novel was merely an episode, if an interesting one, in the literary history of our time. Perhaps this may prove to some extent a universal trend, even if in most countries it is not as yet apparent. . . .

I think that the key to the Swedish experience lies in the fact that, as Holmqvist points out, the emergence of the proletarian writers coincided with the so-called silent revolution. As with so much of Italian neo-realist writing after 1945, the subject matter of the proletarian novelist was largely autobiographical or documentary. It seems probable that the basic difference between Swedish writing today and the so-called proletarian literature of the 1930s arises not so much from the younger generation's different social background as from the nature of their firsthand sources of experience, which were scanty and soon exhausted. If this is correct, Holmqvist's argument is ambiguous because it presupposes that class is determined solely by economic factors. The Swedish educational system (under which secondary schooling is compulsory and access to institutions of higher learning relatively easy) breaks down or diminishes the barriers that used to separate the formally educated man or woman from the self-educated; but it cannot abolish differences of sensibility and mental outlook between people of the same class, nor can it "socialize" that special relationship between mind and reality in which every genuine vocation to art or literature has its root. Moreover, the spread of education has coincided with the prevalence of experimental forms in modern art, as also, at the opposite extreme, with a return to representational forms and classicism. The effort, therefore, of adjusting to his new milieu may easily lead an artist or writer of proletarian origin to adopt a language different from that of the ordinary people, his own former workmates included. He is then himself part of the cultural question mark and not its answer.

Nevertheless it would be absurd to deny that social factors do to some extent condition culture; equally, there would be no point in my venturing into the jungle of surveys and statistics that exist to prove it. For the purposes of my present argument I shall merely attempt to show that, in the sphere of the creation and perception of human artifacts, the relation of cause and effect is never constant, and may sometimes be actually reversed.

The story of mass education during the last hundred years is a case in point. When European liberals and democrats first launched their campaign against illiteracy, many conservatives were frankly terrified. The stability of the existing social order required that the poor should remain ignorant; of this the conservatives were convinced, and their conviction was shared, though from a diametrically opposite standpoint, by the revolutionaries of their day. "Education will set you free," the Socialists of the First International used to preach to their audiences of illiterate working men, "Knowledge is power." The premises of Italian labor organizations were frequently adorned with posters that depicted Progress as a woman with a lighted torch, the symbol of Education, dispelling the darkness of Ignorance and showing priests, in the shape of bats, put to flight by her approach. The most authoritative Catholic organ, *La Civiltà Cattolica*, which was (and still is) under the direct control of the Holy See, took this threat seriously and proceeded to denounce the idea of mass education. "So you want to have a better life?" it apostrophized the working classes. "Well then, work hard and keep away from vice. Production needs no books; what it needs are strong arms and willing hands." In 1876 the *Civiltà Cattolica* defined compulsory primary education as a "fearful threat to order and society."

For a while Education and Progress became synonymous

terms. In the more backward regions of Europe, the spread of revolutionary ideas kept pace with that of education. We know from the Russian novel of the nineteenth century that the Czarist police considered it a felony to teach peasants the alphabet without special permission, and schoolmasters guilty of this felony were deported to Siberia. A Spanish court of law sentenced Francisco Ferrer to execution by a firing squad for having attempted to spread modern educational principles.

Only a few decades have passed, yet it is already plain that mass education has lost its magic and even some of its usefulness. How did this happen? To find the answer we need only glance at a newspaper stand or a bookshop window. Reading, like so much else, can serve not only to elevate the mind but also to debase it. Education is now widely regarded as a means to an end. The dream that leads many low-income families to cripple themselves financially with the fees of secondary or university education is that of seeing their children climb into the white-collar or professional classes.

Even today there are backward parts of the world where to combat illiteracy is still frowned upon or regarded as outright subversive. But, generally speaking, the question of mass education is no longer a matter of controversy. Where controversy continues to rage is in the field of the mass media—movies, radio, television. And, because it is virtually impossible to pass judgment on questions so complex and elusive, they are bound to remain controversial for some time to come. Anyone closely integrated in the life of a social group will find this abundantly confirmed by his own experience: he will soon observe that the influence exercised by the press, television and advertising varies from person to person and that people sometimes remain entirely unaffected by them and change their attitudes for purely idiosyncratic reasons. I am not suggesting that the phenomenon as a whole should escape critical attention—only that any such appraisal is bound to be provisional and incomplete. Let me describe a few situations in which my personal experience has been at variance with the theories current among sociologists.

I have, for instance, always been inclined to take with a grain of salt those sad tales about the loneliness of country people who have migrated to the city. I will readily admit that occasionally one does meet lonely cases, but anyone who imagines them to be the general rule has never really experienced the patriarchal life of a rural society; nor can he have the faintest notion of how often life in one's native village, bedeviled by the ever-watchful eyes and malicious tongues of the neighbors, can become unbearable. Most of the farmers and country artisans who have settled in the city regard their present "solitude" as a merciful deliverance. For many of them it was a deliberate choice to come to the city even though leaving the village meant resigning themselves to a lower standard of living, especially where housing was concerned. The fact that, once they had settled down in the city, the first thing they did was to seek out other people from the same village, is no sure sign of homesickness. If things are going well, if a man who had never before driven anything more mechanical than a donkey cart, now owns a little Fiat, if his daughter has a good job as salesgirl in a department store, he will naturally want to recount these triumphs to an admiring audience. But these old neighborhood gatherings take on a very different meaning when renewed in the city. Living at a safe distance from one's former neighbors, being free to choose those one likes and to avoid others, being able to conduct one's private life remote from prying eyes and wagging tongues—all this combines to give these new bonds of neighborhood a very different character—freer and more spontaneous than the traditional *mores* of rural society. It is almost invariably the women who take the initiative of urging their fiancés or husbands to leave the village, for the principal victims (as well as the principal sources) of neighborhood gossip are, of course, the womenfolk.

It is sometimes argued that, by fostering passivity, conformism and mental lethargy, the mass media are a hindrance to free and democratic practices. This, I think, is unfortunately true, and it is also true that they can pave the way for dictatorships. All the more reason, therefore, to value any evidence that points in the opposite direction.

It is, for instance, simply not a fact that the majority of people vote in accordance with the opinions of their daily paper or the views fed to them on television. In those European countries where there is a wide range of political parties, what happens is very often precisely the opposite. (One need only contrast the large readership of the famous Liberal newspapers with the handful who vote Liberal at election time.) That seemingly docile and passive people have such reserves of psychological self-defense is something that deserves more attention than it has been so far accorded.

I found unexpected confirmation of this in a social welfare project which was carried out in one of the mountain villages of my native region, the Abruzzi. One of the tasks assigned to the young social workers who conducted it was to put on two film shows each month for the benefit of the villagers: one for adults and one for children. They decided to begin with easy films and to proceed by gradual stages to more difficult and sophisticated ones. The original plan was that each performance should be followed by a discussion; but feeling that this might prove too much for the shy villagers they decided on a different approach. It would be better, they thought, if the people who came to see the film were first left alone to talk about it among themselves; later, one of the social workers would visit them in their homes and try to glean their comments and impressions.

Despite all the careful planning, the project proved a failure. The village people produced none of the responses that the social workers had anticipated. No little groups of spectators lingered on after the film show to exchange views; nor could one overhear discussions of the film in the market place or in the tavern. Reaction was nil. When one of the team finally ventured to express surprise at this strange lack of interest, a local inhabitant provided the explanation. "You know how it is," he said. "One sees so many different things nowadays."

Perhaps the future of the human race will ultimately depend on this instinctive tendency of human beings to resist indoctrination, however well meant or disinterested it may be. "One sees so many different things nowadays"; but fortunately it is always possible, even while keeping one's eyes on one thing, to think about something else.

Appearances, therefore, can often be deceptive. Up till a few years ago political problems used to arouse the most heated passions in our young Italians. Today, to be interested in such matters is to be no longer "with it." The younger generation has found other and more absorbing pursuits. Football pools, pop records, television and motorcars have ousted politics from their conversation. This is undeniably a fact. But to avoid overestimating its significance one should pause to consider the real nature and extent of their previous "interest" in politics. For some years after the liberation of Italy, the whole of Italian society was involved in and dominated by politics to an altogether exceptional degree. For many people those were years of fear in which politically compromised officials were purged from their jobs, property was requisitioned by the Allied Military Government and fortunes were lost or made. They were also years of economic stagnation and widespread unemployment. That people flocked in such extraordinary numbers to join one or the other of the political parties, or its youth movement, or its women's movement, and worked actively in it, was a sign of the insecurity of personal and family life, of the growing role of the State in economic and professional matters, and that of party rule within the State. Membership in a political party was sought primarily as a kind of insurance policy, to avoid being "purged" or otherwise discriminated against by the new regime, and also, where possible, as a passport to climbing onto the right bandwagon, getting a job, making a career.

The major political parties were consequently crowded with

people who had no real interest in politics and to whom party programs and party philosophy were a matter of supreme indifference. If a crisis occurred in the party leadership, the sole concern of these people was to remain on the side of the majority. Thus they came to provide a kind of ballast that guaranteed the stability of the party machine. But as the years went by, fear and insecurity gradually gave way to economic resurgence and, with it, the value of political opportunism began to fade. The change has been more clearly apparent in the younger generation simply because they could make it with fewer inhibitions than their elders. The Communist student organization which dominated the major Italian universities throughout the postwar period, has now been dissolved. But even the hard core of Communist Party leaders, in whom a genuine passion for politics has always been the driving force, are now beginning to show signs of a creeping skepticism to which Khrushchev's ideology of affluence has failed to provide an answer. Prosperity is all very well, they say, but then what?

A survey of the moral and religious state of Italian labor, conducted in 1960 by Catholic Action, would seem to confirm this process of regression. One priest who made a study of the workers in the Olivetti factory at Ivrea summed up his conclusions in these words:

Today our Number One enemy is no longer Communism; Communism is suffering from exhaustion. Its propaganda has lost all incisiveness and has ceased to be effective. It has no causes to fight for. The mass membership and mass support that rallied to it fifteen years ago more out of opportunism than conviction, have dwindled away; all that remains is a small group of diehard party workers. . . . Today the Number One enemy in social as in religious questions is apathy and indifference.

To prevent further losses of membership and support, the Communist Party stalwarts are behaving exactly like priests of some religious sect in a period of decline: they continue to enact the ancient ritual while regarding ideological heresy and laxity of conduct with an indulgent tolerance.

5. What Are the Prospects?

Many of the existing divergences of opinion about the affluent society arise from a divergence of viewpoints. One gets an entirely different impression of social reality according to whether one is observing it from without or whether one is actively involved in it. To contemplate it from an ivory tower, apart from being ridiculous, can only result in a distorted vision. The first requisite for understanding any society is that one should not feel alien to it. For better or for worse, this muddled world we live in is the only world we have, and we cannot behave as though we were looking down at it from another planet. The only problem that really matters in the long run, even for intellectuals, is to know what line of conduct to pursue within the limits imposed by circumstances.

At the same time, we cannot remain indifferent to the concern being widely voiced by many thinkers and scholars about certain trends that have recently emerged wherever a society has become prosperous. Social security and mass civilization lead to an increased alienation of the individual, to red-tapism and passivity. But while these facts may give legitimate cause for alarm, they also show us where our responsibilities begin. We cannot adopt an attitude of fatalistic resignation merely because things go wrong. No predicament, however desperate, can deprive us of the power to act. Even in Hell (not that I believe in the existence of Hell, but supposing it did exist, and that it were assigned to us by divine decree) what could we do but try to change it? This is why the current panic about the so-called "hidden persuaders" strikes me as absurd, irrespective of whatever its factual basis may be.

It is argued that social and economic security abolishes, or at any rate diminishes, the element of risk, thereby abolishing or diminishing one of the incentives to enterprise. But what kind of risk are we talking about? Risk is a value only when freely accepted. Prior to the existence of social security legislation this was hardly the case with manual workers, liable as they were at any moment, through sickness or some other misfortune, to find themselves out of a job or actually in the gutter. No indictment of the drawbacks of prosperity is likely to inspire a nostalgia for poverty in anyone who has ever experienced it. Criticism of the affluent society is legitimate as long as it is aimed at such targets as indifference and self-complacency, as long as it serves to remind us that all progress must ultimately be gauged by the increase of man's freedom and moral stature. But it is wrong and absolutely indefensible if it belittles the importance of the partial victories over poverty that have already been won, and discourages the attempt to win them in underdeveloped countries that are still wrestling with the problems of hunger and disease.

The age we live in offers only one sane alternative to the catastrophic prospect of war: that of prosperity for all nations. Reading certain pessimistic diagnoses of the affluent society, one gets the impression that the authors have no conception of what it means to be really poor and miserable. The hedonism of the idle rich can be repulsive, but we should not forget that people who are deprived of life's necessities can be reduced to a state of animal obsession in which they can think of nothing else. If one is always having to worry about unemployment, the grocer's bill, the cost of getting one's shoes resoled and how to keep warm, there is not much room left in one's mind for loftier ideas.

The brutish apathy to which people may nowadays be reduced by the misuse of leisure cannot be any worse than that which was formerly the lot of the manual laborer whose twelve-hour working day left him no leisure at all. The same may be said of the current complaints about social insurance. Its red-tapism is admittedly often deplorable, but the days are not so long past when a worker disabled by a factory accident was automatically reduced to beggary. Italian workers had a saying: "Better dead than disabled." Anyone visiting a shrine or place of pilgrimage in a Catholic country fifty years ago would have found there a swarm of unfortunate wretches, all of them blind or maimed or crippled, dragging themselves around in the dust, imploring alms; and had the visitor bothered to inquire into the origin of their injuries, he would have discovered that the majority of these beggars were factory hands or farm laborers who had been involved in accidents while on the job. Such memories, while they cannot, of course, justify the bureaucratization and all the other shortcomings of socialized medicine, do nevertheless make it impossible to feel regret for the past. Similarly, while we may, and indeed must, deplore the conformism fostered by radio, television, movies, the yellow press and advertising, we should never deplore it to the point of feeling nostalgic for illiteracy. The conformism born of poverty and total ignorance was incomparably worse. Belief in sorcery and witchcraft was hardly less indicative of mindlessness than the reading of comic strips. Moreover, we need not even go very far back in history to point the contrast; in many of the ex-colonial countries of Africa and Asia, as in certain regions of Southern Europe and of South America, the grim realities of poverty are still there for all to see.

All the claptrap about the virtues of poverty is an odious falsehood. But neither should we attach undue significance to the fact that, even with a background of economic security, some people continue to have grievances. If they complain of being unhappy, that is their affair, but then they have no right to expect that prosperity should bring them happiness. What we call happiness is a personal thing, almost always of brief duration, and well beyond the power of any social order to grant or to guarantee. All that can be expected even from the best possible social order is the abolition of such external obstacles as impede man's normal development: political tyranny, racial and religious discrimination, and all the other causes of inequality or injustice. Nothing more.

Here we must frankly admit that once a country has reached, or is on the eve of reaching, prosperity, its situation tends to become pretty much the same whether its regime be New Deal

Democrat, Social Democrat or Communist, and the foregoing strictures apply to them all. Equally it may be said that with the advent of prosperity, under whatever regime, the ideal of progress suffers a moral decline. Does it really make any difference to the life of a worker that he is employed by a State-owned rather than a privately owned factory? A few courageous Polish revisionists have admitted that the "difference" is a piece of pious fiction. An ideal that, having claimed that it would transform the entire range of human relationships, lets its vision of the future dwindle to the boosting of production and consumption figures, has obviously relinquished its meaning. Its symbolical trappings—name, anthem, flag—become mere cultural relics, a mockery of the past.

The entire tone of intellectual life at the present time is adversely affected by the pre-eminence now universally accorded to production and consumption records and by the lack of any longer-term perspective. (All things considered, it is no wonder that among Soviet writers the item whose consumption rate is soaring most rapidly should be vodka.) Jean-Paul Sartre tells us of a remark that was made to him by an official Soviet writer: "When the era of universal prosperity dawns, mankind will at last be confronted with the tragedy of its limitations." The Soviet writer's words would have been even more to the point if he had said: "Marxism will at last be publicly confronted with the tragedy of its limitations." In any case, the sentiment he expressed is an, as yet, only whispered confession of the intellectual bewilderment that has been spreading among the Russian intelligentsia ever since Khrushchev announced the imminence of the propitious-tragic event: the advent of prosperity for all. May the gods assist. In addition to all the obvious human reasons, we have one important intellectual reason for sincerely hoping that Khrushchev's prediction may be punctually fulfilled. Its realization would give us all a single front on which to fight: criticism of the depersonalized, bureaucratic world. The mental outlook—a typically bourgeois one—of those self-styled revolutionaries who now run the lives of the Communist countries can already be seen in all its pettiness. Since their view of history was geared to the dynamism of the underprivileged masses, the threat of imminent prosperity has made them lose their bearings. Their ideology has shown itself to be threadbare at the very moment when it appeared to be close to victory. But what of the future?

The same question is already beginning to arise in some of the more advanced countries of the West, and as the spread of prosperity removes the sources of discontent, sooner or later it is bound to arise everywhere. Yet nothing could be more absurd than to suggest that this will mean the end of historical development. It is true that prosperity eliminates some of the toughest problems that have for centuries tormented human beings and driven them forward; yet, at the same time, it creates or revives others, particularly the problems of culture and society. No one in his senses is likely to expect that even the most widespread prosperity will fulfil Marx's Utopian prophecy that mankind will eventually pass from "the kingdom of necessity to the realm of freedom. . . ." It is impossible to think of a society which has not been born of certain given conditions or is without conflicts; all we can hope for is that the conflicts will be less inhuman and the conditioning factors lose some of their crudeness.

At any rate we know that technological progress does not automatically bring with it progress in culture or morals. It is a pity that many thinkers, by relegating to the sphere of individual psychology all evidence of this unequal development, ignore the dilemmas which arise from it. The typically bourgeois expedient of assuming everything connected with personal life to be a "private matter," and heaping it on the shoulders of the psychiatrist, the confessor or the pedagogue, is utterly pointless. Breathing, too, is a "private matter," but it is not much use trying to breathe in an airless room which has no windows.

A clear insight into this moral dilemma, with particular

reference to the form it takes in countries where the standard of living is highest, has been shown by those intellectuals who maintain that the whole idea of progress needs rethinking.

Some prospect of the future is indispensable to the mental balance both of the individual citizen and of society. But the term "progress," having latterly, and with good reason, become suspect, we nowadays tend to speak of "development," which conveys the idea of change without being loaded by value judgments. From Condorcet to August Comte and Marx, the concept of progress, insofar as it refers to the history of man, has been so often belied by events, that anyone venturing now to reaffirm it can at best hope to evoke compassionate smiles. We may still talk of progress in the natural sciences and technology, but not in the humanities, at any rate not if progress is assumed to be inevitable, for there can be nothing inevitable about matters involving the human mind and heart. There is now a general consensus of opinion that human behavior is neither wholly conditioned nor wholly free. Under any and every regime, the course of human existence will continue to be beset by conflicts and struggles of which the outcome can never be certain. And the "progress" of civilization will always be something to be fought for and never to be taken for granted.

With the coming end of the present phase of economic and political development which has brought prosperity to a number of countries, and in its wake the symptoms of fatigue, boredom and apathy which are being so widely deplored, we are faced with the question how, in such circumstances, any idea of further progress can arise, and what kind of social dynamism will actuate it. For those who like to project their own desires into the future, the quest will present few difficulties. But in reality the shaping of a progressive ideal is always an extremely complex affair in which, around the nucleus of a principle opposed to the established order, there converge personal grievances, unsatisfied needs, material and moral demands of every kind.

There seems to be apprehension on all sides as to where the Soviet regime is leading Russia. In the early years after the Revolution, those who did not believe in the stability of the new regime used to talk of restoring the old order. But they have long since fallen silent: the Russia of today is no longer Holy Russia, and no restoration, not even a purely Socialist one, could find room for the fifty million workers and technicians now employed by State industry. With all respect to the intellectual sagacity of Western Sovietologists, it must be said that they have badly failed us by refusing to look at Russia's future and suggest at least tentative alternatives. The same embarrassed reticence is to be found in the current phraseology of anti-Soviet propaganda. Thus, while the Soviet leadership, in homespun sallies, enjoys predicting that, sooner or later, the West will come to a bad end, no Westerner dares to retaliate by drawing a horoscope of what is likely to become of the Chairman and his colleagues once every Soviet citizen is assured, not only of food, lodging and clothes but also of, say, a bicycle, to put it no higher.

The seeming tranquillity, even monotony, of life under regimes—whether of the Social Democrat or the Soviet type—which have attained a measure of social security might lead one to think that in such an atmosphere the quest for a new principle of progress could only be arbitrary and artificial; but if one observes such regimes attentively from the inside, one will soon notice significant symptoms of conflict. One such instance is the rivalry between politicians and technocrats, and it seems likely that this and other conflicts of the same kind will ultimately be absorbed into the more general antagonism that is now emerging between society and the bureaucratic state.

In totalitarian regimes this conflict is especially evident because the autonomy of the executive at the expense of society is frankly admitted to be a part of official policy. In the totalitarian state the spontaneity of social life is smothered, then revived and recast in the official mold. But the antagonism arises even where a liberal-democratic regime, without being formally abolished, drifts into a centralized bureaucracy. Despite the multiplicity of political parties and the freedom of the press, State control tends to invade all important sectors of public life, especially the economic sector, under the mask of Socialism or socialized Christianity. Political parties, trades unions, cultural institutions also become bureaucratized and financially enslaved, and thus gradually removed from the direct control of their members.

This is not the place in which to discuss the beneficial part that bureaucracy played in coordinating individual effort and bringing the blessings of civilization to certain backward parts of the world. It is true that efficient administration may yet have a part to play in underdeveloped countries whose preponderantly illiterate or semiliterate population is as yet unequal to the responsibilities of self-government. But whether these merits be genuine or exaggerated, there is no reason to assume that government by bureaucracy, even with the guarantee of social security, is the final, let alone the perfect, form of social organization. Any such idea has already been disproved by events: wherever bureaucratic hegemony is most extensive, social rethinking can be seen at its most intense. There can be no other rational explanation of the ferment that has, for some years now, been stirring in the new Soviet generation. As a result of industrialization the opinion-making section of Russian society has grown vastly more important and complex, but it is still held fast in the strait jacket of an anachronistic state.

Thus in the conflict between State and society is to be found the answer to the question: "And then what?" For this is the question that is now being asked both in countries where social reform has been gradual and peaceful and in those governed by a Soviet type of regime. One answer one may safely predict is this: society will attempt to reclaim those of its functions which have been usurped by the State. In all probability the conflict will be long-drawn-out and complicated. Two of the most significant factors for this gloomy forecast are that certain anti-State forces still exist within society; they are survivals of precapitalist times and may fairly be dubbed reactionary. Second, the condition of apathy to which mass civilization has reduced the majority of people is not easily overcome. A society which has put itself to sleep will be slow in turning itself into a free and active community.

There would be no point in closing our eyes to these difficulties, but it would be equally mistaken to consider them insurmountable. The idea of progress is not properly rethought if one merely gears it to new social pressures without human awareness being effectively involved in it. This is not an act of faith on my part; to realize the truth of it, all one need do is to acquire a tolerably up-to-date knowledge of political anthropology. Nothing is more misleading than to reduce the image of man to his digestive or sexual functions. Reality is more dramatic, more complex and more uncertain. Man is capable of revolt both under conditions of satiety and under conditions of want and oppression. Whoever denies this human faculty denies the dignity of man and equates him with the beasts of burden. Of course no law, divine or human, can guarantee that man's revolt will end in victory. But this is one of the risks it is his duty and privilege to take.

But whether the conflict between State and society be slow or rapid in its development, and whatever aspects it may assume in different environments, in seeking one's bearings it should not be difficult to discern the direction in which the hope of progress lies. All one need do is to hold fast to the ancient and welltried criterion: in every age and in every kind of conflict, progress is to be found only in what promotes the freedom and responsibility of man individually and in his complex relationship with his fellow human beings.

1965